# THE SOUL-DIER
## Battling the Unseen

# THE SOUL-DIER
*Battling the Unseen*

*Jason Gregg*

Pleasant Word (a division of WinePress Publishing, PO Box 428, Enumclaw, WA 98022) functions only as book publisher. As such, the ultimate design, content, editorial accuracy, and views expressed or implied in this work are those of the author.

ISBN 13: 978-1-4141-1526-9
ISBN 10: 1-4141-1526-1
Library of Congress Catalog Card Number: 2009906739

# CONTENTS

## PART IV: FIGHTING THE GOOD FIGHT

# ACKNOWLEDGMENTS

FIRST, I GIVE God all praise and glory for this book and for my life. I am here only because He has allowed me to be.

Secondly, I thank my wife, Natalie. You are a rock! You had me at "pompous and arrogant." When my faith stumbles and I lose sight of what is important, you make me smile and bring me back to reality. You make me laugh and find joy daily. You truly are a blessing, inspiration, and gift from God; and I love you more and more each day. To my daughter, Kyleigh, you provide me with joy and a deepened desire to keep fighting. Seeing your smile, hearing your laugh, and watching you grow up make me want to fight the good fight. My daily prayer is that I am on this earth to be with the two of you until I grow old, to see Kyleigh graduate from high school and college, and to walk her down the aisle (with an approved guy, of course).

With deepest sincerity and appreciation, I thank my parents and brother for loving me and joining me on this journey. Your love and encouragement are appreciated. I want to thank my men's group from Pittsburgh—you guys got me through a lot and still hold me up in your prayers. I love you guys and look forward to my return trips for our dinners out and more "prayer retreats." Let's go get some Maryland fish! I also want to give thanks to my small groups in Charleston, South Carolina. You are all like brothers and sisters to me, and I love you all. Our life here in South Carolina is great because of you, and I look forward to going through more of life with you.

I want to say a word of thanks to the two churches that have made a significant difference in my life. Thanks to Northway Christian Community in Wexford, Pennsylvania (*www.northway.org*) and also to Seacoast Church in South Carolina (*www.seacoast.org*). These churches have instilled in me a foundation set upon the Rock. This foundation has strengthened me so that when the storms of life (struggles, battles, exacerbations) have come, I have had the tools to make it through and survive.

Thank you to my doctors, surgeons, and nurses at the University of Pittsburgh Medical Center. Your God-given talents and experience do not go unnoticed and unappreciated. As I battled through trials and pain, you were very patient and kind. Also, thanks to my caretakers at the Medical University of South Carolina. I am so blessed with a great group of docs, nurses, and therapists.

Finally, thank you, the readers of this book. My hopes and prayers are with you and your loved ones, and I hope you find purpose and joy in life.

# INTRODUCTION

I HAVE READ many books in my life and often wondered why they were written. What inspired the authors to write what they did? What experience in their lives took them down the road to make them want to write? I am writing this book because I think it is important for people to understand the variety of issues that people with disabilities and disease face—issues that are not always visible to the eye.

I have a "hidden" disease called cystic fibrosis (CF). This is a chronic, life-threatening, genetic disease that causes mucus to build up and clog organs in the body (particularly the lungs and pancreas). When the mucus clogs the lungs, it can make breathing difficult, and it also causes bacteria to get stuck in the airways, which can cause infections. I was diagnosed with this disease at birth, and today only 18 percent of my lungs continues to work. It is hard for me to walk up stairs or move in and out of different climates. I have frequent coughing spells, am short of breath all the time, have sore muscles (because they are overworked to aid in breathing), use oxygen all the time, and am frequently on antibiotics (both oral and intravenous).

The life expectancy for those with CF is thirty-seven years. I am now thirty-three. CF is a hidden disease, meaning you wouldn't see my disability just by looking at me. You wouldn't be able to see my struggle to breathe or the way my heart overworks to compensate for low oxygen levels. You wouldn't know that I have been hospitalized twice in the last year for infections and that the doctors have told me I won't be alive in two years unless I undergo a double-lung transplant. Yet I am no different from millions of other people in the world with similar unseen disabilities. It is this population to whom I want to bring focus and awareness—to let people know that there is a lot more to those with disabilities than just what meets the eye.

As a culture, I feel we tend to get caught up with the visible and only identify with what we can see. Research states that one out of every five individuals has a disability that would indicate that diseases and disabilities are all around us, but we often do not see them or realize just how close they are to us[1]. We notice a wheelchair or a prosthetic limb but not a person's kidneys or blood sugar.

I am a counselor by trade, and I believe that this, combined with my disease, has given me a unique perspective on the struggles people with disabilities face as well as the strategies needed to overcome them. I want to be a supporter and encourager to those who live day in and day out with a disability and to their caregivers and loved ones. For this reason, I will use my own story, along with the stories of others with similar unseen disabilities, as a platform to try to inspire and educate you to thrive in this world despite any restrictions you might have.

The individuals who share their stories in this book are vulnerable. They show their fears, worries, passions, and successes. It is my hope that these stories will inspire you to look at life through new lenses and learn to accept any limitations you may have and use them for a greater purpose. It is my desire to capture the emotions of these people and allow you to see through their eyes, breathe through their lungs, walk in their shoes, and feel what they feel. Hopefully, this will develop in all of us a new sense of empathy for what we cannot see.

I have a passion and a heart for those who live with a disability *because I am one of them*. I do not want to live a wasted life; therefore, it is my goal and desire to use my disability to bring awareness, passion, and encouragement to others. I wish to provide hope, insights, and tools to those living with disease and show those who do not that what they see in these individuals is just the tip of the iceberg. I want people to realize that in each of us there is a story behind our actions and behaviors, so that we can all become more empathetic toward each other—and maybe even part of the solution.

*Part I*

EMPATHY

*Chapter 1*

. . . . . . . . . . . . . . . . . . . . . . . . . . . . . . . . . . . . . . . . . . .

# WHAT YOU SEE IS *NOT*

# WHAT YOU GET

I T IS ESTIMATED that 54 million individuals in the United States have a disability[2]. That's one out of every five. Look around you the next time you are out and see if you can recognize the one with a disability. Odds are that you will not.

People tend to identify others by what they see. They say things like "Joey always jokes around" or "Phil is always so serious" or "All Cathleen does is work." What they often fail to identify is what caused that person to get that way or what his or her soul is crying out to be. The same is true for people with disabilities. Those with disabilities are often identified by their disability rather than by who they are and the abilities they possess.

Of course, some people who have a disease wear it on their shoulder and choose to make it their identity. As someone with a disability, I am conscious of how easy it is to fall into this trap. I am very aware of my limitations and restrictions, of what I can't do, of what I used to be able to do, and of what I want to be able to do. It's easy to be angry about it, but I can't choose to focus on what I can't do rather than what I can. I have to visualize the positive in every situation and take note of the abilities I have.

It takes time for a person to shift his or her thinking process this way, especially when he or she is in the midst of a storm (such as an exacerbation or recent diagnosis, for example). I've always believed that when a door closes, a window opens. This belief was formed in me from a young age because of the positive influence and Christian morals my parents instilled in me. This postulate leads me to believe that when an individual loses something (such as a skill or body function), he or she has the ability to gain something in lieu of what he or she has lost. It's essential for that person to discover that open window in order to find purpose and fulfillment.

## Understanding Limitations

Healthy people take their health for granted. I see it every day when I go out to the mall or out to eat. If people understood the importance of health, there would be less obesity, less smoking, less drinking, less gambling, and, overall, less negative actions that hurt their bodies and minds. Those of us who suffer from disease and disabilities rarely take a healthy body or even a good day for granted. I praise God on the days when I feel well because I know that tomorrow may not be the same. As a person with a lung disease, every time I see someone smoking, I want to go up to the person, take the cigarette out of his or her mouth, smack that person upside the head, and say, "Do you have any idea how good you have it?" I long for the day when I can breathe without cause or awareness—to just do it without struggle.

We get only one body in this world, and it amazes me when I see people abusing it. When I see people smoke, I feel an internal anger because they are killing themselves voluntarily. What I wouldn't give to have their lungs! If I had good lungs, I would take care of them by not smoking and by exercising. Each of us is mandated to take care of the body God has given to us. First Corinthians 6:20 says to "honor God with your body." If we are blessed to be healthy, we can't take this health for granted and choose to smoke or do other unhealthy behaviors.

One night when I was at the hospital, my wife and I left my room for a walk. As I wheeled my oxygen tank down the sidewalk, we passed a group of nurses sitting outside *smoking*. Here I was wheeling a life-saving oxygen tank around with tubes up my nose, and these professional and intelligent health care professionals did not even consider for a moment that they were killing themselves. Sad!

I tend to be a bit stubborn and do not want to admit the losses I have incurred as a result of my disease. I have had difficulty coming to terms with my limitations, and in fact it has only been in the last few years that my thinking on this has begun to change. Just last year, I had to admit that I could not continue working because it was becoming too difficult. I struggled with knowing that down the road I would need to undergo a double-lung transplant to have any chance at a continuation of life, unless a miracle occurs.

I am scared, although I have not been able to admit this until recently because of pride. Pride can be a funny thing. Of course, I am scared to undergo a surgery in which doctors will cut my chest open, take out two organs, and give me some new puffers (my word for lungs). The funny part is that I am not scared of dying or even of the pain of surgery (although I am certainly not looking forward to it). Rather, my primary fear lies in leaving my wife and daughter. I am scared that if I am no longer around, I will have let them down. I am scared of not seeing my friends. I am scared of not seeing my family. I am scared of not going to church. I am scared that I won't be able to make a difference anymore. I am not scared of dying, but I am scared of not living.

My friend Zena suffers from advanced-stage lupus, an autoimmune disease that strikes the internal organs. She also suffers from heart failure and is in need of a heart transplant, but because of the lupus she is not an eligible candidate. At thirty-four Zena has had to come to terms with her limitations and losses. This once-outdoors gal—a white-water rafting guide, camper, skier, and world traveler—is now pretty much restricted to her house. She is no longer able to work because of her racing heart and the constant pain and dizziness she experiences every day. Zena, and 54 million others like us, and I face life-or-death decisions, pain, nutrition and rehabilitation issues, side effects from medication, unemployment, financial stressors, guilt, and so much more that healthy people cannot understand.

## What Do You See?

I am five-ten and weigh approximately 135 pounds. I have short brown hair and a little stubble on my chin. I have a lanky appearance and am relatively good-looking. (Good self-esteem or arrogance? You decide.) If you passed me on the street, you would not see much else.

If you saw me at church, listening to the message or singing during praise and worship, you might decide that I am a religious person. If you saw me talking to friends in the lobby after church, you might conclude that I am a social person. If you saw me on the golf course, you might find that I really stink at golf (which is true). Or if you saw me at the local coffee shop as I am sitting in front of my computer typing away at this book, you might think that I am very studious. If you got to know me a little bit, you might decide that I am assertive and confident—maybe even a little cocky or arrogant (but I don't think so). You might find someone who is not afraid of a little confrontation or an argument, especially if I feel I am right. All these assumptions would be strictly based on your eyes, and your perception would be based solely on what is visible to you. But is what is visible really reality?

We all see what we want to see and assume what we want to assume based on appearance and visual cues. Many of our assumptions are also based on our past experiences. For instance, if you know someone who is a daredevil on a motorcycle, you might assume that all motorcyclists are careless and reckless. Likewise, if you knew someone growing up who tried to "bring you to Jesus" every day, you might believe that everyone who goes to church is a religious zealot. What you take in through your senses and filter through your past experiences might lead you to a conclusion about a person that has no basis in reality.

We've all heard the expression that there is more to a person than meets the eyes, but how often do we really consider what that means? Our vision can be limited, yet it seems to be the one sensory organ with which we gather the majority of our information about people. In many ways, it can be compared to an iceberg. The behaviors we see in a person are like the tip of the iceberg, while the bulk of what actually constitutes that person—his or her family, culture, religion and health—lies unseen below the surface.

Allow me to illustrate my point. Let's say you are driving down the highway when a lady cuts you off, forcing you to slam on your brakes and swerve away suddenly. What do you think about this lady? Do you automatically conclude that all women are bad drivers? Or maybe you see two teens who belong to a minority walking down your street with baggy jeans and hats turned backward. What do you think about them? Do you get worried and lock your door? Do you think they are in your neighborhood to break into your house or car and cause damage? Do you automatically assume all minorities are criminals? Do you think they might be in a gang?

What about a guy who has feminine qualities? Do you automatically assume he is a homosexual? Do you think horrible things about him and call him derogatory names? Do you do this in front of your children? What about a teacher who yells at a student or, heaven forbid, your child? Do you think, *How dare she,* and automatically conclude that she is a horrible teacher who hates your child? After all, who is she to talk to your child that way? Your child told you that he or she did not do anything to warrant such a confrontation, and you believed it.

## What Do You Not See?

There is always a story behind every action. Maybe that woman who cut you off on the highway was a single mom who was just let go from her job. Or maybe she just received a phone call that her sick mother had been rushed to the hospital and had only a few hours left to live. The two minority teens you saw may live in your neighborhood or the neighborhood next to yours. They may be involved in their local church youth group and in honors classes at their school.

The guy you met with feminine qualities may be straight, married with children, and a good father. He could not help the way he was born. Or maybe the guy was sexually abused and is unclear about his sexual identity. This may be his way of coping. The teacher who yelled at your kid might have been justified because your child (as innocent as you think he or she is) inappropriately touched another student or cussed at the teacher. Or maybe the teacher just found out that she does not have a job next year and is overstressed (as most teachers are). Haven't we all had a bad day and responded the wrong way?

Before we are so quick to judge others, we need to realize that we are just viewing the tip of the iceberg—that which is visible—and basing our assumptions on life experiences and mental beliefs we picked up earlier in life. We tend to jump to conclusions based solely on what we want to see and want to believe. We fail to recognize that the person who is walking slowly in front of us and delaying us from our schedule could be in pain and is walking as fast as he or she can go. The person looks so normal on the outside—but inside he or she could be suffering greatly.

That tip of the iceberg (what is visible) makes up only 10 percent of who we are. Where does the other 90 percent come from? It comes from inside our minds and hearts. It's comprised of our experiences in life, our upbringing, and our religion. It consists of our sense of right and wrong, where we live, our choice in friends, and our sexual experiences. It's formed from the abuse we may have suffered earlier in life, the church we grew up in (or didn't grow up in), the teacher or youth counselor who made a difference in our lives, or that family vacation we took, when we realized how much our family loved us. These are the things that have developed us into who we are today. It is all these experiences, life situations, and so much more that have created the 90 percent of the iceberg lying under the surface, which displays itself through our actions and behaviors.

## Keeping Up Appearances

As a culture, we are quick to judge others. But do we really want others judging us based on what they see? Some people go to great lengths to make themselves appear perfect on the outside, but inside they are torn into a million broken pieces—so much so that they walk through life with a blindfold on as to who they really are. They are not willing to take a good look at their interior lives (their souls, minds, hearts, values, moral systems) as long as they "appear" to be with it. After all, isn't image everything?

Have you ever walked into a person's house and found it immaculate, but then opened a closet and found it stuffed with junk and odds and ends? Everything on the outside looked perfect until you took a deeper look. Hollywood is a good example of this. Celebrities spend a lot of money, buy homes in the elite areas of the country, drive the best cars, and take vacations to exotic places in the Caribbean. But then we hear about the substance abuse, the latest divorce, the children born out of wedlock, the amount of community service they owe, the twenty-four-hour marriage in Vegas…the list goes on. The song "Celebrity" by Brad Paisley pokes fun at celebrities because of their attitudes and the efforts they take to appear that they have it all together. The song goes on to say how they appear completely normal, but their appearances do not match their internal selves.

Are these people content and happy? Have the money, houses, cars, and clothes brought them peace in their lives? Maybe or maybe not, but my guess is that the majority of these celebrities are not clear as to who they really are. They spend a lot of time and energy to have that tip of the iceberg show what they want to show, but not who they necessarily are on the inside.

Abraham Maslow's hierarchy of needs puts self-actualization at the top of the pyramid as the final destination or ultimate accomplishment in life. What is self-actualization? My own definition is that it represents the point at which what is on the outside matches what is actually on the inside and we have joy, peace, and harmony in our soul. It means that despite all the things that have happened to us in life, we have come to a place where we accept life as it is and find purpose in living fully and serving others with the gifts we are given.

Remember, even those who have experienced losses from a disease still have gifts. These gifts, just like the muscles in our bodies, will atrophy if they are not used, but with time and hard work they can be redeveloped. It's never too late to start, and those with disabilities need to redevelop and redefine their gifts based on their losses. People with disabilities have a story that is not always visible on the surface. We must take the time to get to know them and understand their diseases to truly have any inkling of what it's like to be in their shoes. Once we begin to understand what they experience day in and day out, this knowledge will help us live life with more appreciation for what we do have, rather than for what we do not.

Simply put, what you see is not necessarily what you get. As a counselor, I tend to listen more to what is *not* being said than what is. As the old adage goes, "Actions speak louder than words." Usually, what a person is saying to me is only the tip of the iceberg—there is much more that lies beneath the surface, and it can sink that person's ship. Many times, I have students walk into my office and tell me that everything is "fine," but their body language, grades, behavior, and choices say something completely different. "Fine" is the standard answer when you don't want anyone to ask probing questions or investigate any further. What they are really saying is, "I am in a lot of pain, but I'm scared to be vulnerable and truly tell you what is going on."

Unfortunately, because our society has instilled in us the idea that vulnerability and showing emotions are weaknesses, we have been trained to hide these things. We put on a front or mask and say that all is fine and that nothing is bothering us. I have seen some kids and adults who are dealing with an astounding amount of pain, but despite what is going on, they still feel the need to show face and remain steadfast. We learn from a young age the law of evolution—that only the strongest survive. I believe vulnerability and survival go hand in hand. In fact, I prefer to think of survival in terms of "thrival." I want to thrive in this world despite living with a disease that makes it difficult to just survive at times. In the same way, all of us need to ask ourselves what we want in life: to just survive or thrive.

## Looking Past the Surface

If you were to look at me, what you would not see is the feeling I have of someone sitting on my chest all the time. I hide my symptoms very well. You would also not be able to see my fears and worries. However, they are nonetheless very real in my world. All individuals with unseen disabilities have similar real and scary symptoms they must deal with on a daily basis—symptoms that cause a lot of issues and struggles in their lives.

There are many diseases to which we as a culture do not pay much attention. My hope is that as a culture we will begin to gain more understanding of and empathy for those with disabilities and find ways to be more genuine with our neighbors, colleagues, and friends. It is my hope that we will begin to comprehend that when we look at people, we may not always know what they are dealing with in their lives. What we see is not necessarily reality, but looking past what we can see is the beginning to gaining understanding of where people really are.

## Chapter 2

# THE IMPACT OF DISEASE

B Y THE TIME I reached six months of age, the doctors knew something was wrong. I was not growing adequately in weight or height, so they did a slew of tests and ultimately confirmed that I had cystic fibrosis. They labeled me as "failure to thrive" and gave me a life expectancy of nine years.

I was blessed to come into this world as part of a Christian home. When my parents heard the diagnosis, they told the doctors that I had been born into the right family and that they would love me and take care of me regardless of any physical issues I had. And for the most part, I had a normal life growing up. The only abnormal parts included taking pills with every meal to help me absorb food and the breathing treatments I had to undergo twice a day to keep my lungs free of infection and to get the excessively thick mucus out of my lungs.

## Cause and Symptoms of Cystic Fibrosis

As I mentioned in the introduction, CF is a genetic disease. To have CF, a person must inherit two copies of the defective gene that causes the condition (one from each parent). If both parents carry the CF gene, their child will have a 25 percent chance of inheriting the two defective copies of the gene that causes the condition.

Their child will also have a 50 percent chance of inheriting just one defective copy and being a "carrier."

According to the Cystic Fibrosis Foundation, approximately thirty thousand people in the United States have been diagnosed with CF. At least ten million more—about one in every thirty-one Americans—are carriers of the defective CF gene. The disease is most common in Caucasians (in fact, it is *the* most common genetic disease among Caucasian children), but it can affect all races. Currently, there are one thousand new cases diagnosed each year, and the current median age of survival of someone born today with CF is thirty-seven years[3].

One of the main issues with CF is that it causes thick and sticky mucus to build up in the lungs. Although there is some debate about what causes this condition, scientists believe that it goes back to the defective CF genes in the person. Typically, a healthy CF gene makes a protein called CFTR that controls the movement of electrically charged particles in the body. When that protein is defective, the salt balance in the body is disturbed, and there is too little salt and water on the outside of the cells. The thin layer of mucus that aids in keeping the lungs free of germs becomes thick and extremely difficult to cough out.

This thick and sticky mucus lines the airways of the lungs and makes it extremely hard to breathe. Because it is so difficult to cough out, bacteria (or germs) get stuck in this mucus, causing inflammation and infections that ultimately lead to lung damage. The mucus can also block the digestive tract and prevent the body's natural enzymes from getting to the intestines. This is why I have to take oral enzymes to aid my body's absorption of food. Unfortunately, they do not work as well as my body's natural enzymes. I do not digest my food well, and as a result I have low bone density (osteoporosis) and difficulty gaining weight due to malabsorption.

Many of you reading this are probably thinking that it would be great not to be able to gain weight. But one person's joy is another's battle. I am skinny, and this has led me to be self-conscious of my appearance. All my life I have heard comments about my weight and have had to endure nicknames such as "green bean" (which is what one friend used to call me). Adding to the problem is the fact that people with advanced-stage lung disease like mine can use up to five thousand calories a day *just breathing*. When you combine this with the problem of poor food absorption, and when you add in the amount of coughing I do, it is no wonder that I have trouble gaining weight and am often fatigued.

## Living with Cystic Fibrosis

I mention coughing because it is a big part of my life. I cough frequently throughout the day to try to force out the thick and sticky mucus that blocks my airways. It is a major aspect of my story with CF, and it is chronic, which means it only worsens over time. To the average person, my cough sounds really nasty. It causes some uncomfortable moments for me when I start coughing out of control in public and people think I'm dying. It's awfully embarrassing. I have learned to stifle my cough to avoid making a scene so I don't draw attention.

The only way I could really describe to you what living with CF feels like is to have you imagine that you had asthma and had to go through the day with a clip on your nose as you breathed through a straw. The disease is constant in my life and affects every part of it. As I mentioned earlier, I am down to 18 percent lung functioning, which means that 82 percent of my lungs does not work. Because of this, I get short of breath with minimal exertion. In fact, it's hard for me even to walk up a flight of stairs without getting out of breath. It's hard for me to go out and wash my car because the physical exertion requires moving my arms up and down in order to wash it. It's hard for me to tie my shoes, because bending over cuts my oxygen levels and causes me to become lightheaded.

I have learned to avoid stairs and hills and to make excuses as to why I cannot go somewhere or do something, even though I would love to go. (My wife makes fun of me because I'll drive around a parking lot for ten minutes until I find a close parking place. I don't want to walk very far for fear of being out of breath and coughing.) When I walk up to my bedroom on the second floor, I have to take a moment to catch my breath. When I go downtown to walk around, I often have to take a break every few hundred feet because I am struggling to breathe. I choose restaurants that do not have stairs and try to pick vacation cities that are flat so that I do not have to climb too many hills. I feel self-conscious when I travel or go to visit friends because I have to take my large, heavy oxygen machine to help me breathe when I sleep, along with lots of medication and a nebulizer breathing machine that helps the inhaled medications get to my lungs.

My back and shoulders hurt most of the time because my body has physically altered itself to provide the maximum amount of space in my chest for my lungs to expand. This has given me a "barrel chest," and I wear loose-fitting clothing to hide this condition. The physical adaptation also causes strain in my back muscles, which in turn causes me to have frequent headaches. In addition, when I go to the bathroom, it smells like raw sewage because my body absorbs so little nutrition. As a result I go to the restroom two or three times each day. The smell makes me self-conscious. One time I went to a beach house with friends for a weekend and was so paranoid that I would smell up their whole house that I "held it" as long as I could. At other times I have avoided going to the bathroom for so long that it hurts. This is not recommended.

I don't like hotels because I have developed a bit of anxiety about germs. I worry that I will get sick and that the sickness will develop into the next lung infection that lands me in the hospital. In fact, I'd rather drive home eight hours than spend another night at a motel to avoid being exposed to germs. Please understand that when most people get sick with a bacterial infection, they can simply go to their local doctor and get an antibiotic, but in my case—because of the number of infections I've had over the years—most oral antibiotics do not work. They are just not strong enough to kick an infection, and I often require IV antibiotics to fight it. For this reason, I also worry when I hear people coughing behind me, because if they are sick, I might catch what they have and end up in the hospital.

CF affects every single aspect of my life and is on my mind from the moment I wake up to the moment I go to bed. I have to deal with it all day, every day, with no mental or physical relief. It's constant. I am aware of just about every breath I take, and I usually have to force that breath. I carry around my oxygen tanks and tubes so that I can have a constant flow of air to keep me up to par on the breathing field. Doctors tell me that after my transplant I will have to relearn how to breathe because I've forced my body to do so for so many years. I look forward to learning this and having a lot more energy to do the important things in my life.

## The Realities of Living with Disease

It seems to me that CF receives little media attention, which is unfortunate because it is more prevalent than many people think. Most of the diseases that get attention in the media today are the ones that have suddenly afflicted some Hollywood celebrity. CF, on the other hand, is different because there is no sudden onset. Those with CF are born with it, and because of its severity, few people make it to adulthood.

It's a sad truth that people with CF do not generally live beyond their thirties. I recently lost a thirty-one-year-old friend to this dreadful disease. I am also familiar with an eighteen-year-old who is suffering from severe rejection.[4] This disease is age ignorant, and exacerbations occur differently in everyone at any age. Currently, there is no cure for CF, but specialized medical care, aggressive drug treatments, therapies, and proper CF nutrition can lengthen a person's life.

These are only some of the issues of living with a chronic disease—a condition most people never even consider. Life with such a disease takes top priority for the person who has to endure it. In my own situation, I know that I have to take extra care of myself so that I have the time and energy to be a dad and a husband. In this chapter, I've shared some of the issues I've had to deal with due to my CF, but there are hundreds of other diseases and disabilities out there that affect people in a variety of ways. There is no such thing as a "textbook case." Symptoms differ between people, but one thing is universal: loss and suffering.

*Part II*

# OVERCOMING

# Chapter 3

## MAKING LEMONADE

I F I'VE HEARD it once, I've heard it a million times: "If life gives you lemons, make lemonade." My mother shared this golden nugget of information throughout my life, and she continues to say it to me today. Yes, it drives me nuts, but as much as I hate to admit it, maybe my mother knew something I did not.

At some point in all our lives, we receive bad news. We get what I call "lemoned." This bad news may involve failing a class in school, losing a job, suffering an injury to a child, finding out that a friend has been diagnosed with a disease, experiencing the passing of a loved one…or anything else that causes grief and disruption in our lives. For my parents, receiving the news of my diagnosis when I was just six months old represented a major "lemon" in their lives. Bad news is hard to hear, and nobody is ever ready for it.

### Getting Lemoned

Psychiatrist Elisabeth Kubler-Ross identified five stages of grief: (1) anger, (2) denial, (3) bargaining, (4) depression, and (5) acceptance. Whenever a person receives tragic news about a health issue, he or she goes through each of these stages. In fact, a person cannot truly accept his or her new self and find purpose in it without going through this process. I have been lemoned throughout my life regarding my disease, but recently I went through a situation that took me through all five stages at once. The lemon I received shook me to the core and made me feel as if I had been hit over the head and in the gut with a two-by-four.

This bad news came in the form of the negative results I received from an echocardiogram I had received a few weeks before. The doctors had heard a heart noise during the exam and felt that I might have pulmonary hypertension. In short, they were concerned that the blood pressure in my lungs was too high and that my heart was struggling. When I later called the office for my results, the nurse told me, "The doctor will call you personally." Now, if you've ever heard those words, you know it's usually not good news. Good news is when the nurse says, "All your tests came back normal."

Later, I spoke to the doctor over the phone. "Less than two years to live," he said. Those words resounded off me like an echo in the Grand Canyon. It was as if all the air in my lungs (which was not that much) was pumped out of me. I wasn't ready for the news, and I was breathless. All I could hear were the words "less than two years" over and over in my head, like a broken record.

As it turned out, when the doctors conducted the echocardiogram, they discovered that the pulmonary hypertension was a lot worse than they had originally thought. The doctor told me that normal pressure in the lungs is between twenty and twenty-five. Mine was around 59. Ouch! More than double the norm! I could barely speak, but somehow I managed to have a conversation with the doctor about my options. My fears were finally coming true: I needed to move forward with a lung transplant.

I empathize with anyone out there who has ever had a similar experience because it was one of the worst episodes I have experienced in my life. Here I was, a thirty-two-year-old guy with a wife and daughter, and the doctor was telling me that by the age of thirty-four I would not be with them anymore. When I later called my wife at work, I could barely speak because I was so devastated. I had never before let anyone hear me cry the way I did that day, but the floodgates just opened and the tears flowed like a river. It was as if all my thirty-two years of coping skills had gone on strike and I had nothing left, so I just let it out.

My friend Zena experienced a similar situation about a year ago when one of her doctors—who, I might add, had horrible people skills—told her, "Get your affairs in order because you will not see your next birthday." Imagine the challenge that held for her. She was in her early thirties, had a career, and was falling in love with a guy she was dating. What does she say to the guy? How do you tell someone you love—someone with whom you are thinking about marriage and a future together—that you have less than one year to live? Put yourself in those shoes for a moment and try to see how that would affect you. What would be your next action?

## No Guarantees

Once I had recovered from the initial shock, my thoughts moved to what I would do about the transplant. I already knew the statistics for the success rate of that operation, and they scared me, but it at least would give me a couple more years—or so I hoped. (There are no definites in life). Research says that the survival rate for a person who undergoes a double-lung transplant is, on average, about 50 percent at the five-year mark.

Choosing to undergo the operation may sound like an easy decision to make, but when life-and-death emotions are on the burner, nothing is ever easy. I had to ask myself, *DO I want to go through the difficult and painful process of having the transplant without any guarantee that it will work?* Are there ever any guarantees in life? As a professional counselor, it is easy for me to give advice and have insights into other people's struggles, but it's very difficult for me to take my own advice and listen to my own insights. I had a huge life-or-death decision to make, and I was scared.

One thing I have learned from life experience and from being a counselor is that you should never make a big decision—especially a life-and-death one—based on emotion. I call it the "heart-mind" battle, because one of them usually wins over the other. When you make a decision based on emotions, the one that usually comes out on top—the heart—is wrong. God gave us a brain to reason, think, and rationalize through issues. Our heart goes immediately to what we want, not necessarily to what is best for us. Our emotions tend to lead us to what is easy and what gets us the most satisfaction the quickest. It's great when these two areas are aligned, but that is not the norm. So I knew that I had to use the brain God had given me to make this decision, because if I left it up to my heart, which was reacting to the fear I was feeling, I would have made the wrong one.

## Making Lemonade

I had been lemoned, and I needed to make lemonade. One way I have found to do this is to confront the fear with prayer and ask God to help me focus on the positive in the situation. What can I take away from this experience? What is the take-home lesson? I have also found it important to read the Bible to learn about God's character because His character is love. I'm so grateful for His love because out of it He extends grace and mercy, which is something we all need. The Bible is full of directives, promises, teachings, and lessons that can help us overcome and redirect our thoughts.

One of the books I used to help me during this time was *The 4:8 Principle: The Secret to a Joy-Filled Life* by Tommy Newman. The 4:8 Principle is based on Paul's words in Philippians 4:8, which states, "Finally, brethren, whatever things are true, whatever things are noble, whatever things are just, whatever things are pure, whatever things are lovely, whatever things are of good report, if there is any virtue and if there is anything praiseworthy—meditate on these things" (NKJV). It's about finding the joy that God has already given us and learning how to tap into it. The 4:8 Principle helped me to realize that I should not meditate on fear or worry but focus my efforts and energy on the positive. I wanted to thrive, and in order to thrive, I could not give fear and negative thoughts any space in my mind or heart. I had to replace it with joy and positive thoughts, just as Paul teaches in Philippians.

It took me a lot of tears, sleepless nights, fears, worries, and talks with my wife and prayers. But after the initial shock, I eventually decided to follow the 4:8 Principle and focus on being joy filled.

This was not an easy transition to make, but it was well worth it. Here's how I ultimately rationalized the decision-making process for the transplant in my mind:

> *I am thirty-two, with a wife and daughter. With good health I could have a fulfilling career. I have so many great friends and a wonderful family. I do have a lot to live for. My biggest heartfelt prayer is to grow old with my wife and see my daughter graduate and even get married. As of this moment, the doctors tell me that I have less than two years to live, so I have to take that at face value. If I move forward, face my fear (and pride), and get the transplant, I have a fifty-fifty shot at living five more years. I guess that's better than a 0 percent shot at five years if I do nothing.*

I know of a mother and father who made a poor decision not to pursue a life-saving procedure for their daughter. I think they let fear win the battle and thought they could use alternative processes to cure her. Unfortunately, they lost the battle and, ultimately, their daughter. At the funeral, the father said, "I had no idea it was this bad." I did not want my family giving a similar testimony. I needed to do everything in my power to continue to be a husband and a dad for long as I could, and that meant fighting the good fight, facing my fears, and enduring a painful process, with the hope that the end would justify the means.

It was time to face my fear and move forward with confidence. I had been living a life paralyzed by fear, and I needed to face the future with an attitude of hope and expectancy and get on the transplant list. I realized that I could only speculate about what would happen once I had the operation because I was not in control. Rather, God is in control, and He does not have to speculate about the outcome. I needed to be a positive thinker and place my trust in His ways and stop believing that my way was better. It wasn't!

## Facing Your Lemon

My friend Zena has to face her lemon every day. She knows that her heart could give out at any moment, leaving her husband a widower. Another friend, Leslie, lives with chronic pain. Roger was diagnosed a year ago with an incurable lung disease, and his insurance is fighting him on getting a transplant. George, at twenty-five years of age, has survived cancer and has a new liver, but he wonders what will happen next.

None of us feel sorry for ourselves. We continue on in life, fighting for what is important. Even though we get lemoned a lot, we choose to make lemonade. We literally fight for each day because our families, our faith, and our friends are worth every medication, every needle stick, every biopsy, every fear, and every moment of pain. Courage is facing that illness, that decision, that fear, that *lemon*...and moving forward despite the odds. We can do this only by choosing to change our perspective, by deciding to focus on what we have and can accomplish rather than on what we have lost, and, most importantly, by surrendering our situation to God and trusting in His plan.

What is your lemon? What has you so wrapped up in fear that you are unwilling to take that next step? What do you need to do to change your perspective and turn that negative into a positive? I am able to face my lemons only by trusting in God's goodness and grace. God only gives good gifts, but I think we need to take that leap of faith in order to receive them. So I encourage you to stop allowing fear to envelop you. I encourage you to begin to step out into uncertainty and see what God has in store. It takes a lot of prayer and courage, but it is worth it.

# *Chapter 4*

# SURVIVAL VERSUS
# "THRIVAL"

I SHARE MY story with you so you can understand that having a disability affects every facet of my life. When I wake up in the morning, I do not say what *should* I do; rather, I ask what *can* I do? It's a different way of life and one that most people do not grasp unless they experience it firsthand.

One thing I have come to realize is that many who suffer day in and day out do not complain about it. They may go to work every day in constant pain, yet their colleague in the cubicle next to them has no idea that they are suffering. They have come to realize that complaining does not do anyone any good, especially themselves. They do not like to draw attention in such a way as to elicit sympathy, and they never want their disability to become an excuse. I saw this recently when I was in a pulmonary rehabilitation program. Every person there was either going to need a lung transplant or would probably not be on this earth in five years, yet not once did they complain or feel sorry for themselves.

Most people I have worked with had no idea of the difficulties I endured on a daily basis. Once when I told a colleague that I was going on disability, out of pure ignorance she said to me, "Oh, I wish I could go on a permanent vacation like you." I wanted to smack her upside the head and say a few choice words, but I refrained. Another time, a colleague said to me, "You look fine; you should be at work." I responded with "It's not what you see, but rather what you don't see." It's what you *don't* see about a person that matters. It's what lies below the surface that often writes the stories of our lives.

Each of us needs to be more empathetic with those we see around us. After all, the person sitting next to us at the coffee shop or the woman selling us a book may be in pain. They may be struggling to breathe, anxious about surgery, or suffering from a multitude of other symptoms that are all hidden from the eye.

## An Issue of Attitude

Most of us allow life to pass us by without taking a moment to stop and smell the roses. I know this is a lame cliché, but I say it because I believe people with disabilities typically adopt one type of mindset or another: they allow the disease to beat them down, or they accept it and appreciate what they have in life. It's an issue of attitude; they either choose to be beaten down or to overcome. They either choose to *survive* or to really *thrive*. And when they choose to thrive, they find a new purpose and meaning in their situation.

I believe that within every disability, ability is reborn. I think of people who have lost their vision or are born blind. Even though they have lost their sight, their bodies have made accommodations by increasing their sense of touch and smell. They see; it's just through different means than those with physical sight. As I have said before, when God closes a door in life, He opens a window. When we lose one ability, we may be able to find another, but we have to have the right attitude for that to occur. We have to look for the positive in life and not let our circumstances beat us down and keep us from moving forward.

Whenever I am waiting in the hospital or at doctors' offices, I make it a point to observe those around me who are suffering from the same disease I am. I can usually tell the ones who have allowed it to overcome them because they will just be sitting there, looking miserable and sad. Some of them even stink of cigarette smoke—and if you have a lung disease, the last thing you want to do is smoke.

As I mentioned, my friend Leslie lives in severe pain much of the time. She has been to many doctors and homeopathic therapists, but nothing has helped. Yet despite this, she has not allowed her disease to overcome her. If you watched her walk down a flight of stairs, you would notice that she takes each step a bit more slowly and holds on to the railing a bit more than you would, but you would not realize that every step she is taking is causing her pain. She works for a living, takes care of her family and home, eats right and exercises, does not smoke, takes vitamins, goes to church (which is good for the body, mind, and soul), and has many friends. She is trying to take care of her one body on this earth and is making the absolute best of what she has. She is thriving despite the pain she is living in day in and day out. She is an example to many of how to live despite circumstances.

Likewise, my friend Zena has not allowed life to overcome her despite some very difficult circumstances. Currently, she has to temporarily move away from her husband and head south because the cold weather is hard on her. Her husband has to keep working up north and plans to head south to see her as often as possible, but unfortunately the economy is dictating some of their actions. She is also trying to get evaluated at a large hospital in the hope that she can get into a federal study, which may grant her the opportunity—and maybe her only chance—for a heart transplant. If this hospital does not accept her, her only chance for a transplant is to go to Germany. She would probably have to pay close to a million dollars for a procedure that *may* provide her with a few additional years with her husband.

## Beyond the Physical Battle

For me the decision to go on disability and pursue the transplant option was a difficult one to make. The mental, emotional, and spiritual battle that ensued became a larger and more difficult struggle to overcome than even the physical one. I was suddenly confronted with the realization that my life was going to change forever and that I would experience some sort of loss. Here's an example of some of my internal battles:

*I am thirty-two and have a wife and daughter. We live in a nice house, drive nice cars, and have a comfortable lifestyle. Doctors have told me that I have less than 20 percent of my lungs working and that one more bout with an infection could end it all. Now my heart is being affected, too, and the doctors are saying that I have less than two years to live.*

*If I choose to forgo work and go on disability, am I giving up? Am I allowing this horrible disease to win? Am I letting myself down and admitting that work has become too hard for me to bear? Am I being selfish by choosing this route? If so, why should my family have to suffer for my disease? They have not done anything wrong, but their lifestyle will change because we will lose my income. I won't get to take my wife on a cruise like I had hoped to do again because we won't have the money.*

*And how do I tell my parents that I am leaving work? All they'll hear is that my health has declined and that I cannot work anymore. They'll automatically assume the worst and believe that I am worse off than I really am. How do I tell my boss and colleagues? What will they think? What will my new purpose be if I cannot be a school counselor? Where is God in all this? Do I have the faith I should? Why is fear controlling me so much?*

Every one of those thoughts were (and are) real to me. They represent real struggles, sorrows, questions, and fears I had to deal with as I went through this process. This same sort of internal battle can flare up in anyone who has to live with an illness or who has to face a difficult crisis. At some point, each of us has to ask tough questions of ourselves and of God.

*Why me, God?* We've all asked this question before. I heard it from a number of people in interviews after 9/11 and Hurricane Katrina. I heard it every day in my counseling office when a client would walk in with a crisis on his or her hands. I heard it from parents when their children were misbehaving and doing some pretty bad stuff. I've said it myself numerous times. We all have.

During one of my low times when I was experiencing some serious pain, I told God that I hated Him. I was angry at Him. Anger is a normal emotion that often results when we are experiencing fear. It is also a powerful emotion that has the ability create a lot of pain for ourselves and others if it is not handled properly. I have since asked God for forgiveness, but I still get angry at times and go through periods of depression and frustration when I seem to be more angry with God than at other times.

The funny thing is that I have never blamed God for giving me this disease. I was born with CF! God did not give it to me, and neither did my parents. However, even though I have not blamed God for it, I have been angry with Him for *not taking it away*. There is a big difference there. I know that God can intervene (and I realize He already has, or else I would not be here today to write this), but at times I still become angry and doubtful of His goodness.

## The Road Less Traveled

I believe God is an all-powerful, all-loving, and all-knowing God. Now, you may be asking how an all-loving, all-powerful, and all-knowing God would allow me to have CF. Likewise, why would He allow my friend Zena to have lupus and heart failure and my friend George to have liver disease? Why does He allow *anyone* to suffer?

I am no pastor or theologian, but this is how I have come to understand it. In the beginning God made a perfect world, which started in the Garden of Eden. He created this dude, Adam, and this chick, Eve, and they were married. Everything was great. But then Satan tempted Eve, and she pulled Adam into the situation. Well, at that moment sin entered the world, and God allowed pain to enter as well. He did not force pain on people, but rather allowed it to happen.

So pain and suffering are just things that each of us, as members of the human race, have to confront. They are the realities of our existence. And in many ways pain serves an important function—it brings us awareness that something is wrong. It gives us motivation to change. Have you ever allowed your child to learn a lesson the hard way so that he or she would not do something again? It's the same principle at work here. I believe how we live our life is a choice. God gave each of us free will, and we can choose to live life either for a greater purpose or for ourselves. And when we choose to live for ourselves and let our circumstances overwhelm us, we will have to suffer the consequences for our decisions.

A good friend of mine once said that life is like middle school. As a middle school counselor, I have to agree with him. I see far too many adults being narrow-minded and focusing only on themselves and the immediate issue they are dealing with (whether good or bad). They feel that every little crisis is the biggest thing in the world, and they take the victim-mentality road rather than accept the responsibility. I notice that it is not uncommon for people to gossip a lot, make others look bad, take the easiest way out, and overall be dramatic. All these characteristics are stereotypical of the middle school generation.

We all have a choice: we can take part in this negativity and egocentricity, or we can try to take the higher road. There are times when we will get sucked in and enter the drama of life (like middle schoolers), but we should always try to take the road less traveled—the road where we do the right thing because it's right, not necessarily because it's easy. The easy way is not necessarily the right way.

In my own situation, I know that I can choose to be angry (and stay angry) about my chronic lung disease, or I can choose to *not* make that my primary focus. I can look for sympathy from others, or I can go out and live my life the best I can. I have found that it's best to choose the latter. After all, what has anger and bitterness ever gotten me? What has wallowing in my own self-pity or looking for pity from others ever done for me? I want to live with purpose and passion, and the best way to accomplish this is to focus on the positive, not the negative—to thrive and not just survive!

There are so many things about my life that are good and healthy. So why would I want to occupy all my thoughts and energy on the one aspect of me that is not good—my lungs? I want to be a positive impact on those I come across in life, and to do this, I must work every day on being positive and joy filled.

*Chapter 5*

# CHANGING YOUR GOGGLES

D ISEASE AND DISABILITIES change people and how they view life. They have the capability to creep into a person's emotions, fears, thoughts, beliefs, values, and relationships. They affect a person in unique ways and even change his or her personality.

Some people are healthy for an extended period of time and then have a sudden onset of symptoms and a diagnosis that invokes change in their lives. In my case, because I have never had a disease-free life, I have no way of knowing who I would have been or what I would have been like if I had not been born with CF. For me, growing up with a disease forced me to live in a particular way and see the world in a particular light. My worldview, or way of seeing the world around me, would have been very different if I had never had the disease. But, as that was not the case, I have developed my own set of goggles that were partially formed by the process of disease.

We all wear these "goggles." They are unique to each of us and influence the way we see the world. No one person sees the world as another. For instance, people who grow up in rich families, drive around in Ferraris, and always have the best of everything have a very different set of goggles than those who grow up in poverty.

People who have been emotionally, physically, or sexually abused certainly wear a different set of goggles than those who have grown up being able to trust others.

My goggles are different from someone who is disease free, and certainly different from someone who takes his or her health for granted. However, while I have a hard time feeling sympathy for people who hurt their bodies when they know better, I do have empathy for them because I can relate to their suffering. For instance, when my grandma developed emphysema from smoking two packs of cigarettes a day for fifty years, I could empathize with her suffering despite the fact that it made me angry she was abusing her lungs. All these feelings and perspectives are a part of my goggles, and these goggles are continually being developed and transformed through my experiences and choices.

## Forming the Goggles

Among other things, my goggles were formed through my interactions with my family, my upbringing, my religion, my education, my friends, and, of course, my disease. In many ways, growing up with CF has been beneficial to how my goggles have developed. I feel that it has allowed me to be more intentional with my relationships, more empathic with others, and more willing to enjoy life one day at a time.

My disease has also forced me to slow down, and this in turn has enabled me to appreciate things others often pass by without ever taking notice. I live in one of the most beautiful parts of the country, the low country of South Carolina, where coastal waters meet marshes that extend as far as the eye can see. This area of the country has birds, dolphins, alligators, and other wildlife; thousand-year-old oak trees draped with Spanish moss; blue skies; the smell of the ocean; and so much more of God's wonderful creation. Because of my disease, I have learned to appreciate the beautiful surroundings in which I live and to be thankful for them.

Slowing down in life is a good thing because it forces us to focus on the important things—things such as God, relationships, love, and our true purpose in life. Think about it this way: If I get in my car and drive down a beautiful road at 120 miles per hour, I won't see much of that beauty because my focus will be on staying on the road. In fact, if I'm driving at 120 miles per hour and don't stay focused on the road, I may end up dead. Sure, I will get to my destination quickly, but at the cost of missing the beauty all around me. I believe that beauty—love, joy, hope, peace, friendships, relationships, a good book, a day at the beach, quiet time with God—is a much more important focus than a destination point or a thrill. As my dad always says, "Enjoy the process."

Due to my breathing issues, my disease has forced me to walk slowly. This seems to be a metaphor for my life. If I get in a hurry and walk too quickly or get anxious, this affects my breathing, and I suffer. Slowing down my journey has allowed me to focus more on my soul and on building relationships with others than on material items, which always fade away. That's probably the reason I became a counselor: I feel empowered when I listen to people's struggles and can help them to be overcomers and thrivers. My goggles allow me to help others because I have walked in their shoes and understand at a deeper level what they are experiencing. If I had never been diagnosed with CF, I may never have found this out about myself. I may have been too busy driving at 120 miles per hour and missing the beauty around me—along with my purpose and passion in life.

## The Impact of Worries, Fears, and Anxieties

Worry is a huge part of our society and occupies so much of our time and energy. Yet despite how much of our time it occupies, it's the one thing in our lives that gets us nothing in the end. Think about it: most of the things we do get us *something* we want. We place our time and energy into relationships because we want to get something of it—whether that is friendship or love. We work because we want to live in a house, exercise because we want to stay healthy, go boating because we want to enjoy life, ride a motorcycle because we want to experience freedom, mow the yard because we want our place to look nice, go to the doctor because we want him to stop the pain…and so on. But what do we get out of worry?

Perhaps this is why God tells us to "not be anxious about anything" (Phil. 4:6). But is this reasonable? Is this realistic? I often feel anxious about my health because I know my disease is severe and I will most likely die from it at an early age, thereby leaving my family and friends. I know that CF can and ultimately will kill me, and that plays some real mind games within me. I have mentioned how one of my main fears is that I will not be able to provide for my family now that I am on disability. I also worry about being a good dad and husband when I am not feeling well. I worry about what my wife will do when I am no longer here. The last thing I want to do is hurt her by leaving. I worry about having to get a transplant and the pain that is involved and what I will do if it does not work. These are all valid fears I deal with on a regular basis, and they creep into my mind quite often.

What do you worry about? Fill out the table below by identifying the top five things that cause you anxiety. Maybe they are your finances, your spouse, a friend, your health, your job, a doctor visit, or your children. It does not matter what they are—just think through them and write them down. Then, next to each item, write down what that worry provides for you. In other words, write down what you accomplish or get out of worrying about that thing. Remember, you do everything for a reason, so the challenge is to identify what that worry is providing in your life.

| What I Worry About | The Outcome This Worry Provides |
|---|---|
| 1. | |
| 2. | |
| 3. | |
| 4 | |
| 5. | |

Did you find that worry accomplished anything positive? I hate to be the one to tell you this, but worry will *never* change anything for the good. It only brings stress, anxiety, ulcers, and high blood pressure. It will sometimes even destroy your relationships with loved ones. Worry is based in fear, and fear is often a result of loss of control. What's ironic is that while worry is one of the few things we can control to some degree in our lives, we usually allow it to control us—like a dictator over a country.

## Changing the Lenses

So how do we begin to change these lenses? How can we exercise control over our fears and worries? I have learned that while I cannot necessarily control my thoughts, I *can* control what I do with them. I know that when I allow fear or worry to enter my mind, I have two choices: (1) I can allow it to affect me and win over me; or (2) I can face that fear and not allow it to control me. So when these anxieties begin to creep into my life, I have to change the lenses on my goggles from those of fear to those of hope and joy. That is difficult to do, and it takes a great deal of practice. It has required me to place my hope in Christ and trust that He will never give me more than I can handle.

I believe that what does not kill me makes me stronger. I have survived through every battle and every exacerbation of my disease, and this survival has made me strong. I do not mean "strong" as in physical strength but in terms of character and resiliency. When I overcome, it boosts my faith and increases my tenacity to survive. When I truly release worry, surrender my fears, and give up the control, true freedom begins. Trusting in God's divine plan gives me that freedom, and I have found that when I trust in Him in spite of my circumstances, my faith deepens.

I have also come to the realization that I cannot confront my worries and fears on my own. None of us can carry a mountain load of stress and physical symptoms on our shoulders without help. At some point, it just becomes too heavy to bear. For this reason, it is good to have an "inner circle" of friends or family members with whom you can share the anxieties. This is especially critical if you are suffering from a disability or have a loved one who is.

I have always had a group of men with whom I could be vulnerable about my struggles. I trust these men completely. They accept me, listen to me without judgment, and support me in prayer, love, and friendship. My wife and I also meet regularly with a small group of couples and families to do life together. I find that it is essential to have this inner circle of support and love, for when my "arms" (my emotions and physical being) get tired, this group holds them up for me. When I feel too frustrated to keep fighting, they provide me with encouragement and support. When my fears overcome my faith, they pray for me. When my wife is weary, they surround her and help with chores, meals, and prayer. This group of friends and family is vital to my success, and I love them all dearly.

No one who is battling a disease can do it alone—at least not successfully—but in our culture we often grow up with an attitude of complete independence. "I don't need any help" becomes our mantra. We must give up this illusion of control, for until we do, we will not succeed in thriving.

## Living Successfully

Living successfully with a disease does not necessarily mean we will be healed from it. Rather, it involves identifying what we have—not what we have lost—and making the best of it. It means changing our view from what we feel was our purpose before the disability (or prior to any exacerbations) to a new purpose we can handle more realistically. It means realizing that while we do not control our disease, it also does not control us.

It has taken me a long time to realize this. For many years I tried to control my disease, and when I found that I could not, I would get angry and frustrated with myself and with God. I have since come to realize that while CF will dictate certain things in my life—such as my limitations and restrictions—I have the choice in how I will cope with those things. For instance, it would be completely absurd for me to think that I could run a marathon,

38

since I cannot even run up a flight of stairs without feeling the ramifications of it! So how stupid would I be if I let the fact that I cannot run a marathon bother me or get me angry and upset? I have to come to terms with what I can and cannot do and am at peace with it.

No matter what I do, this disease will continue to get worse, and nothing I can do will ultimately stop it. However, this fact does not entitle me to be miserable or give up hope. Rather, I must step up and do everything I can to maintain my health. By giving in to anger or hopelessness, I only allow myself to go down the path of despair—a path that would change my goggles to an ugly gray color. I want my goggles to show blue sky, sunny days, and a joy-filled vision. To do this, I must release control and accept what I cannot change.

When we do this—when we let our anger go and release our false sense of control—then and only then can we experience freedom and change the lenses in our goggles so we can see our new purpose despite our loss.

## Chapter 6

# THE IMPORTANCE OF FAMILY

D ISEASE ALWAYS INVOLVES some form of loss. It may involve the loss of some function (such as the ability to breathe well or regulate one's blood sugar), loss of freedom, loss of a job, loss of a way of life, loss of mobility, loss of one's senses...you get the idea. When we experience that loss, the first group to jump in and compensate for it should be our family. Knowing our family supports us and loves us no matter what we do or how we live is a key ingredient to good health and development. Family is essential in building a strong sense of confidence and self-esteem within us.

Unfortunately, not all of us come from families who have developed good coping skills or who know how to best love and support us. It's almost as if in our society, the dysfunctional family has become the norm. Many of us have families who have hurt us, and we harbor resentment or bitterness against them. Many of us struggle to be independent from our families. Some of us need to forgive our families to move on, others of us need to accept our families as they are and allow ourselves to love again, and still others of us need to confront generational issues in our families.

One thing I have been forced to learn—and trust me when I say it was a very difficult lesson—is that when one person suffers with a disease, the whole family is part of it. In my own life, I have often tried to carry the burden of my disease by myself because I never want others to suffer or worry because of me. For example, I have lost the ability to go out and mow the yard or do the physical things around the house I used to do, and any time I think I am feeling strong enough to do a chore like this, I usually regret it immediately and for a couple of days afterward.

My immediate reaction to a physical activity or chore is to begin out-of-control coughing. This is accompanied by a panic-invoking inability to breathe, which causes more coughing, which in turn causes me to be even more out of breath. It's a vicious cycle! There are also the unfortunate times when I go too far and end up coughing up blood (a condition known as hemoptysis). Being the stubborn person that I am, I will forgo common sense and attempt this type of activity again, because I don't want to accept my limitations.

I am learning to accept these limitations more and more and, as my lungs have continued to deteriorate, to humble myself and ask for help. I know that when pride begins to rule over me, it will lead to poor health, so I have to force myself to let that pride down. I have to be willing to ask for help when needed, and often my family is the first place I go to look for this. I have learned to accept help from my wife, my family, and my friends because they are there to carry some of the burden for me. After all, that's what you do when you love someone—you help.

I am blessed to have married the most amazing woman in the world. She has accepted my disability and now performs the duties around the house I normally would do. Likewise, my parents often came over and helped out with yard work or other manual duties because they knew my restrictions and wanted to help. It's important for loved ones to be able to help when we need it—and we need to learn to be appreciative of it and accept it with open arms.

## FAMILY DYNAMICS AND DISEASE

Family dynamics are as eclectic and different as snowflakes, and each will have a variety of ways of dealing with a loved one's disease. Take my family, for example. I grew up in a middle-class, two-parent Christian household where I was loved and encouraged to be everything I could be. Having been born with a lung disease, I had an increased level of need, but fortunately my parents had lots of love and care to give. I remember many family dinners, family vacations, soccer games, musicals, camping trips, hikes, and father/son retreats. My family provided me with a stable and firm foundation so I could develop and grow in confidence and self-esteem despite having a chronic illness. Their innate willingness to help me instilled in me a desire to help others.

Two years ago, my wife and I decided it was time to move our family to a warmer climate because the cold air in Pittsburgh was difficult on me. (If you've ever been to Pittsburgh, you know it's almost always cold or rainy.) We were ready for a change. Having to tell my family was challenging because I knew how they would take it. My dad, as expected, took the news relatively well and understood the situation, even though he was disappointed. My brother and I cried together because he and I are very close. I knew he would be angry with God and probably think this would be the last time he would see me, though that was not the case. Telling my mom was also difficult. Mom is emotional and struggles in letting loose the reigns of motherhood, so I knew she would take the move harder than anyone.

Each of my family members, when confronted with the news that we were moving 650 miles away, dealt with it in different ways. And while there is no right or wrong methodology for grieving, there are definite issues that come to the forefront when families are coping with loss. One such issue is boundaries.

## Boundary Issues

Boundary issues tend to be more of an issue with moms. Women, generally speaking, handle life's situations with an emotional ruler. They gauge the severity of the situation and then measure how much emotion they will let out based on the situation. Because situations involving disease tend to be greater in severity than other life situations, they release a greater measure of emotion in those instances—especially when it's a mother/child dynamic.

Boundary issues can be dissected into other areas, such as control, overprotecting, and enmeshment. Let me break these down and identify some ways to deal with each.

## Overprotection

Mothers of "sick" children are notorious for being overprotective. It's innate within them as nurturers and protectors of their children. They learn the roles of caretaker and caregiver at an early age, and they become part of their goggles.

My mom has lots of love and good intentions, but, like most moms, she struggles with being overprotective. Learning a child has CF would be very difficult for any mom, and her immediate reaction would be to want to protect that child from harm, infection, and loss. Protection means survival in a mom's eyes, so regardless of what she perceives is causing the harm, her job is to step in and stop it. This is how mothers are created, and there is nothing wrong with this because children need to be carefully watched and kept safe from danger.

But look at this from the eyes of a child. Every child, regardless of his or her health status, wants to be normal, to be accepted, and to fit in with a crowd. Children with a "hidden" disease—a disease that is not immediately noticeable to others—look completely normal but have certain limitations and restrictions imparted on them by the disease. Mom knows what the child can and cannot do, but the child's friends do not, so Mom takes it on herself to place limits to protect her child. After all, God placed parents in a position of authority over children.

Of course, children do not see it that way. Children often ignore what is good for them and follow the path of least resistance—even if that path is not healthy or safe—to get what they want. They see their parents as dictators who have sovereign authority over them and are just being cruel by saying no. This is difficult for the mother who wants her child to be accepted and involved but who also feels the need to limit the child's activities for his or her own sake. It's also difficult for the child who desperately wants to fit in but has a mother who is saying no.

The hard part about being parents is that sometimes we have to be the bad guy to do the right thing for our children. The trouble comes when we cross the line from protecting our kids to overprotecting them. As parents, we must be willing to let our children venture into the world when they are old enough to do so, even if this involves their failing or getting a little hurt. There is a bit of teeter-tottering here because as parents we must assess the risk level and, if the risk is acceptable, allow the child to learn a lesson by trying something out of the ordinary. This way the child can see whether the activity is beyond his or her scope and ultimately learn a valuable lesson. If the child is never allowed to venture out, he or she will take this sense of defeat and fear of risk into adulthood or, even worse, direct the anger he or she is feeling at the parents.

## Letting Go

Another issue common in most parent/child relationships when a disease is present is letting go. I remember my mom crying out of control when I left home and went to live at college. It was only twenty miles away, but it might as well have been in Siberia. When I later bought a home of my own, she cried hysterically although my new home was less than ten miles away. As is common with mothers who spend their lives being caregivers and providers for children with special needs, she had a hard time seeing me as an adult who was capable of doing things for myself. Through no fault of her own, she viewed me as a little boy with a disease, even though I was twenty-six years old at the time.

Because of these attachment issues, it's much more difficult for parents raising children with special needs to let go. Imagine the empty-nest syndrome times ten. It's a natural transition—and a healthy one as well—but difficult because moms and dads are no longer needed in the same role.

Parents, whether young or old, need to realize there is a point in their child's life when he or she will grow and develop into an independent person. It takes a conscious, deliberate act on the part of the parent to begin the process of letting go of the role of caregiver. As noted, this is difficult but necessary in order for children to learn how to take care of themselves and be less dependent on others for their needs. Independence is essential for individuals with a disability. Being self-reliant builds a stronger sense of confidence and self-esteem within them.

## Enmeshment

"Enmeshment" is a counseling term that refers to an overlap of relationships. The best example I can think of to explain the concept is from the movie *E.T., the Extra-Terrestrial*. In one scene, E.T. is at home and Elliott is sitting in school. E.T. and Elliott have become so connected to each other—so enmeshed—that when E.T. finds a can of beer and drinks it, Elliott gets drunk. Despite their own uniqueness, each was able to experience what the other was feeling.

Think of this in terms of relationships. Individuals with a disease go through a realm of emotions and struggles that are unique to them. Just as no one person is the same as another, his or her struggles, thoughts, emotions, and fears will be very different. However, when a parent and child are enmeshed, they begin to feel the same way as each other and are so interwoven that each identity cannot be separated. When this occurs, the parent or child may feel the need to protect the other from the emotions he or she is feeling.

In my own life, I often felt the need to hide when I was not feeling well to protect my parents from worry. I felt that if I was sick, so were they, and I did not want this pressure and false sense of guilt. This was a self-imposed burden that I carried around for years, and it caused me a lot of anger and stress. It also led me to believe (irrationally, of course) that it was my fault if they became upset over my disease and that it was my responsibility to protect them by hiding my symptoms from them.

For me, this began as early as middle school and lasted through adulthood, when I finally realized that I had become enmeshed with my parents' feelings. After I realized this was not my burden to carry, I released it and told my parents that I had been hiding aspects of my condition so they would not worry. Our relationship improved, and I did not experience the same guilt anymore. I no longer hide things from my parents because I don't feel that I deserve to carry that guilt or feel the need to protect them. How they deal with the news is up to them.

## The Problem of Guilt

Another issue in many families is guilt. Many parents—moms in particular—struggle with guilt because they feel responsible for their child having the disease or disability. This is especially true of parents who have children with genetic diseases, although it's a feeling that is not warranted. Guilt can run deep into the parents' souls and have a lot of control in their lives if they don't deal with it appropriately. It is important for parents to release that guilt and not carry it around.

As I mentioned, CF is a genetic disease I inherited because both of my parents were carriers of the gene. I am not a psychologist, but I believe that because of the guilt my mom has felt over this, she has always felt somewhat responsible for my having the disease. In turn, she has developed some unhealthy coping mechanisms to deal with this guilt. In my mom's case, she covers up her difficulty in knowing how to cope with my health issues by doing things to help her feel needed—primarily by serving others. My mom is that person who will go the extra mile for others. She will serve hundreds of people in need, run a food bank, take on the role as a deacon in church, and help organize a fundraiser. She thrives on serving. Now, while this is certainly a worthy cause, it can also be used as a way to avoid addressing the real issues.

A person can use any cause or activity, no matter how worthy or important, as a means to deny the reality of a situation. Any activity—eating, surfing the Internet, sewing, exercising, volunteering—can become an unhealthy coping mechanism if it becomes a person's sole identity and is used to avoid something. Even a healthy coping skill, if used in excess to live in denial, can turn unhealthy. In my situation, I know that my parents are not to blame for me having CF. God is not to blame. Parents of children with disease—especially genetic diseases like CF—need to learn to let go of the guilt and adopt coping mechanisms that don't involve hiding from the reality of their circumstances.

## The "Fix-It" Mentality

We've listed several unhealthy coping skills that mothers of children with disease often adopt, but what about fathers? Most dads tend to be less emotional and often take on a "well, let's just fix it" mentality. Guys are problem solvers and want to fix the situation. Unfortunately, dads can't "fix" their children's diseases or disabilities, and they will struggle with how to handle the situation. They may want to do more for their children but not know how. As a result, they will tend to avoid the problem by getting lost in work, sports, or fixing the car.

There are many dads who choose to hide from the problem and not do anything about it. This is unfortunate because dads play a unique and vital role in their children's lives by being there for them. All children, whether disabled or not, love to hear from their father, "I'm proud of you," and dads can and should be involved in the care of their children. For instance, when the children are younger, dads should go to the doctor's appointments with them. You may say, "But most dads work and cannot get the time off to go." Well, then fathers must ask themselves what is more important: work or their children. Some sacrifices will have to be made. Of course, this does not need to be all the time, but dads should exhibit a level of involvement that demonstrates they are educated on what is going on and be present if necessary.

As the child with the disease gets older, the dad's role will change to more of a supportive function. However, by staying involved in the child's life, the dad can demonstrate he is still engaged and concerned about that child's welfare. A simple "How ya doin'?" can show a level of care that is not intrusive but still evident. A supportive and educated dad can also aid in the relationship between the mother and the child with the disease. In general, dads have an easier time allowing their kids to make mistakes and learn from them, and for this reason they can help the mom in learning to let go. A mother often feels she is responsible to do it all, and when the man shows a level of involvement, it tells her that she is appreciated and is not alone. Dads can also provide care and encouragement to the mom, who most likely is stretched pretty thin.

## Siblings and Disease

My favorite show is *Everybody Loves Raymond*. In the show, Raymond, the younger brother, receives favoritism from his mother, who is very intrusive and has no boundary skills. As a result, Raymond's older brother, Robert, is often left feeling less important and demoralized. This is all done with humor and makes for a funny show, but it demonstrates some great brother dynamics.

Siblings in families with sick children often get overlooked and left behind. This is not done intentionally or maliciously, but rather because the parents lack the time, energy, or resources to focus on more than the main issue of the disease in the family. Children with special needs require extra care, so when there is a healthy child running around the house, he or she is often given less attention. This occurs to an even greater degree during sick periods or exacerbations of the disabled child, where the siblings are frequently passed on to grandparents or neighbors. This limits their time with Mom and Dad, and these siblings run the risk of growing up with a greater need for attention (which is often sought after using negative means). They may also exhibit lower self-esteem, perform poorly in school, make poor choices in friends, and adopt different sets of social skills.

It is important for parents to understand this issue and make accommodations for all their children. Maybe this means that Dad takes the healthy child to the zoo on Saturday for a father/child day, or vice versa with Mom. It may mean that everyone sits down to dinner together and talks about something other than sick Johnny. Children want and need their parents' attention and affirmation.

My older brother is wonderful and would do anything for me—even to the extent of giving me a lung, as he once offered. I am grateful for my brother and the sacrifices he has made for me. However, while growing up he was a bit rebellious, and I feel this was partly due to the fact that he had a brother with a disease who needed extra attention from Mom and Dad. He had some anger issues and blamed God for my condition, which led to his adopting some poor coping skills. It takes a long time for people, especially families, to let go of the blame and release their anger toward God. Many never do and end up living with anger, bitterness, and resentment.

## Developing Positive Coping Skills

I share this vulnerability about my family to show that people who love someone with a disease tend to cope with it in a variety of ways. Some people cope by externalizing their thoughts and emotions, holding them out there for others to see. Others cope by internalizing their feelings and keeping them locked inside. The particular coping mechanism a person will adopt is usually based on his or her personality. Those whose personality is more extroverted (the outgoing, type-A personalities) tend to adopt the externalizing coping pattern, while the reverse is true for the more internalizing types.

The unfortunate consequence of internalizing is that it formulates anger, which is then expressed in a multitude of ways. Some examples of how this anger is expressed include substance abuse, sexual addiction, excessive behaviors, guilt, self-mutilation, food addictions, physical abuse, outbursts, cussing, violence, passive-aggressiveness, and even mental illness. The funny thing about internalized anger is that it will always come out eventually. It's like holding a beach ball underwater—you can hold it down for only so long until it pops up unexpectedly. Anger is no different; it will show itself eventually in a negative way unless the person learns to deal with it appropriately. This is why each of us needs to establish positive coping skills and lean on family and friends when needed.

For these reasons, family members with a sick child need to develop positive coping skills and learn to handle their emotions in a constructive way. They need to learn how to avoid boundary issues, guilt, the "fix-it" mentality and other improper ways of dealing with a disease in the family. They also need to avoid using worry and anxiety as coping skills. Developing positive coping skills will lead to improved communication between family members, a sense of confidence in being able to handle future struggles, more positive thinking, hope, and a sense of peace. There is nothing worse than going through an exacerbation of a family member's disease with no healthy coping skills.

Chaos is not healthy in a family structure, but if coping skills are not developed, this is usually what ensues. So to keep chaos and fear at a distance, here are some tools you can use to deal with difficult situations and struggles by any family member, whether healthy or sick:

- *Get some alone time and reflect on your reactions.* Are they helping or hurting the situation? Are the reactions too severe for the circumstance?
- *Get a support group.* Find a small group or a few close friends you trust to rely on and talk to (in other words, find an inner circle).
- *Do something you enjoy.* It's easy to get so focused on the storm that you miss the things in life you enjoy. This may include reading a book, journaling, hiking, eating out, biking, or going to a movie. Take time from the chaos to relax.
- *Meet with a counselor or pastor.* These are individuals who are trained to walk with you through difficult times and who can provide tools and techniques to promote health and coping skills.
- *Eat healthy and avoid drugs and alcohol.* By eating healthy, you avoid food and chemicals that are bad for your body. Your body, mind, and spirit are all interwoven and connected. Drugs and alcohol only cover up emotions and do nothing to heal or help. Look at the first tool listed here: are you helping or hurting? Avoidance is never healthy!
- *Communicate.* Do not keep everything hidden inside. If you messed up, ask for forgiveness. If you are hurt, let the person know in a respectful way that you were hurt. Be

vulnerable to those in your inner circle and allow them to walk with you through whatever you are going through.

- *Exercise.* It's good for you and provides your body with natural endorphins that will make you feel good. It is also a great stress reliever.

As a person with a disease, it is often difficult for me to ask for help. I am very independent, but my current health status now dictates that I change that perspective. Interestingly enough, when I put the shoe on the other foot, I realize there is nothing I wouldn't do for a family member or friend if he or she were in my place. Like most people, I like to help because it makes me feel involved and needed. So I have to ask myself why is it any different for me.

My wife and I are so blessed to be surrounded by many loved ones, both family and friends, and they really do make all the difference. I am blessed because I do not need someone to shower me or assist me with personal hygiene, but many people with diseases do, and that has to be very humbling. I am appreciative to the caregivers out there who use modesty and respect in the way they help others. This is what functional families do for each other, and many family members sacrifice their own wants and needs to give care to others. This is the ultimate gift!

## The Support of Family

The day I realized I had found the right woman to marry was the day I told her I had cystic fibrosis. I was honest in telling her the details about the severity of the disease and that ultimately it was chronic and fatal. I was so scared to tell her because in my mind I couldn't understand why someone would want to be with a person who may not be alive in five years or who may have a lot of future struggles. In addition, most CF males are infertile, so having children would take a miracle or an act of science. I don't remember her exact words, but she said she couldn't care less. She had complete faith in God, and this faith overcame my own fears and anxiety. I married an amazing woman, and I am the most blessed man alive for being with her.

I do admit, however, that even though we have been married for five years, I still have doubts. I know my wife is God-given because she is the perfect woman for me and she puts up with my idiosyncrasies, but I still wonder why she loves me and how she does not worry. If I were in her shoes and she were the one with the disease, I would be freaking out and not know how to handle it. She is stronger than I am, and her ability to cope and trust has been a rock of support for me. I believe that in Natalie's heart she thinks I'll be healed. Now, whether that is through a transplant or not, I do not know, but I do love her faith and try to tap into it to help me remain strong.

I also worry about being a good dad. As I mentioned, I am an internalizer, and because anger is part of internalizing, I tend to exhibit that anger toward my daughter. There are times when I am short with her, use the wrong language, or do not spend enough time with her because I am frustrated in other areas of my life. In truth, I am not really angry with her but at the situation I am in. I am unable to be the type of dad I want to be, and this frustrates me. Of course, these behaviors are unfair to her because she has done nothing to deserve my quick temper.

I dream of the day when I can breathe effortlessly and be strong enough to play soccer, ride my bike, go for a jog, mow my yard, and take my wife on vacation (hopefully to Ireland). At times, I feel less of a man because I cannot do these things. My wife tells me all the time that I am the perfect man for her, but I continue to struggle to see myself this way. I know I have many great qualities and a lot going for me, but it is so easy to focus on what I cannot do. It's easy to get stuck in a rut and see only the dirt around me. This is why it is so critical for me to have the support of family and loved ones who will help me live out the 4:8 Principle—to focus on what I can do and lead a joy-filled life.

Families should be the first point of contact when help is needed. Do not say no to someone who is in need. Helping a loved one is not about you, but rather about him or her. Be willing and ready to help out that individual with a need, and do so with a joyful heart. We are set here on this earth to help others, and true joy and purpose come through this. I am thankful to my family for being there during my times of need and for the ways they have encouraged me to be anything I wanted to be—even an author.

# *Part III*
# SPIRITUALITY

*Chapter 7*

. . . . . . . . . . . . . . . . . . . . . . . . . . . . . . . . . . . . . . . . . . . . . . .

# WHERE DOES GOD FIT IN?

I HAVE NEVER hidden the fact that I get angry with God at times. There are even times when I have cursed Him out. I feel that God would rather me be open and vulnerable with Him about my feelings than hide them and pretend everything is great in life. After all, He already knows what is going on in my mind and heart. Psalm 44:21 says that He "knows the secrets of the heart" (NKJV).

As I mentioned previously, the reason I get angry with God is not because I blame Him for giving CF to me (because I do not believe this) but rather because He has not done more to heal me from it. I grew up believing in miracles and healing—it's just part of my goggles—and I know that God has the power to heal any illness. I have often tried to rationalize to God that if He were to heal me, He would get more glory from it than if He allowed me to go through a transplant or continue to suffer. I tell Him, "Wouldn't Your power be magnified to the ends of the earth by showing how You healed someone with an incurable disease? How could anyone doubt You were God after that?" However, I have had to learn to accept that while God has the power to heal me, for some reason He has chosen not to do so at this time.

God does anything He wants (Ps. 115:3), and His ways are perfect. Deuteronomy 32:4 states, "He is the Rock, his works are perfect, and all his ways are just. A faithful God who does no wrong, upright and just is he." Given this, who am I to be angry with God for not healing me if it is in His will? I have discovered that it is always better to allow God to work His plan in my life than to try to force my own agenda. After all, His ways are perfect, so I must trust in that. If I try to glorify God but have an agenda of my own, it opens the door to pride and selfishness.

## God in the Details

When a loved one is suffering from a disease, it is easy to get caught up in the question of where God fits in. Where is He in the situation? The answer is that He is everywhere—He is in every facet of life and in every detail. God is the Alpha and Omega, the beginning and end, and He is in every minute detail of every living and non-living thing. Furthermore, because God loves us and created us in His own image, it is not His nature to give bad gifts. However, if we choose to stay angry with God and not accept His will in a situation, it is easy to miss all the blessings and gifts that He is providing to us on a daily basis.

God has done many miracles in my life and has blessed me immensely. I am alive today, which I believe is a miracle in itself. Every day that I wake up is a gift. Of course, the skeptic may say that I am alive because of science and technology, and I will agree with that statement. However, who do you think created the doctors and the technology? God showed His grace to me from the beginning by allowing me to be born into a godly family with parents who had the resources to take care of my needs and a brother who would do absolutely anything for me. He has opened doors and shut doors for my family and me and has answered prayers countless times. He has blessed me by placing me in locations with incredible doctors who could treat my condition and in cities with excellent health care systems.

God's greatest gift to me was to provide a wife who cares and understands and loves me regardless of what I can or cannot do.

God had pre-arranged the time and place for us to meet, and now we are going on six years of marriage. We have a wonderful, Christ-centered, and self-sacrificing relationship. God knew I was unable to bear children, so it was in His divine plan that when Natalie and I met, she was already a mom to a two-year-old. It took some time for me to adjust to having an "insta-family," but it's something I would do all over again because I now have two of the most amazing women in my life. I never would have known the joy of fatherhood and seen the sparkle in my daughter's eyes and heard the laugh of her spirit had I not met Natalie.

God has blessed me with a group of amazing friends who pray for me, laugh with me (and at me), and cry with me. He has used my illness to His glory by giving me a story that helps me to identify with those who also suffer. He has allowed me to write this book and work with people who need encouragement. Through this disease, I have been shaped and molded into the person I am today. He was in that detail just as He is in all the other details of my life.

Whether or not I could always see or feel His presence when I was going through trials does not negate the fact that He was always right there in the middle of them. It's like the wind—we can't see it, but we cannot deny its power. All these are gifts from God, and I know that I am to be grateful for them and not complain that it isn't "fair" that God hasn't healed me. After all, if we want fairness, what we really deserve is death (see Rom. 6:23). And when I stop to think about it, the only thing really lacking in my life is strong lungs. So why should I focus on what I do not have instead of on what I do have?

We must always believe that God is in every detail, regardless of the circumstances we may be facing. We are here on earth not by any actions of our own but through the grace of God, and for this He alone receives the glory. When our bodies are failing, our souls can still live on, and we must identify how to make a difference in our world so we can follow His purpose for our lives. When we provide a drink to the thirsty or feed the hungry or provide lodging to the homeless, we are doing it for Christ (see Matt. 25:35-40).

## Living in a Fallen World

In John 9:1-3, as Jesus and His disciples are walking along the road, they see a man who was blind from birth. Jesus' disciples ask Him, "Rabbi, who sinned, this man or his parents, that he was born blind?" (v. 2). Jesus answers, "Neither this man nor his parents sinned,…but this happened so that the work of God might be displayed in his life" (v. 3).

I love this story, because here's this guy who was born blind, and he *remains* blind until Jesus heals him. Back in biblical times, it was believed that if you were born with a disability, it was because you did not have enough faith to be healed or because you or someone in your family had sinned. Sadly, some people still believe this is true today. I have heard some people say that they are not being healed because of a lack of faith. I have heard others say that God will not heal them because of their past. I have heard pastors preach that we can have perfect and wonderful lives if only we give ourselves over to Jesus and that if we do, He will give us whatever we want.

A lot of people take Scripture out of context in this way and try to make it say what they want it to say. However, while God gives us the grace and the ability to handle situations that come at us, nowhere in Scripture does it say, "Give yourself to Jesus, and your life will be everything you want it to be." On the contrary, Job 5:17-18 states, "Behold, how happy is the man whom God reproves, so do not despise the discipline of the Almighty. For He inflicts pain, and gives relief; He wounds, and His hands also heal" (NASB). Likewise, James 1:2-3 states, "Consider it pure joy, my brothers, whenever you face trials of many kinds, because you know that the testing of your faith develops perseverance."

God may heal us, but He just as well may not. He may allow a loved one to get cancer and possibly die. Christians are not protected from pain and trials. People who follow Christ die the same way as atheists, Buddhists, Muslims, and those of every other religion. The difference is that Christians have the equipment and tools to handle whatever life gives them. They have the armor of God to protect them and give them strength. They steadfastly hold onto hope and know that there is more to this life on earth. They are able to focus on eternity with Him as their final destination rather than on a hole in the ground.

In my own situation, I know that I have CF because it is a *genetic* disease, not because of a lack of faith on my part or because a family member sinned. Romans 3:23 says, "For all have sinned and fall short of the glory of God," which means that we all sin—but not everyone has a disease. Christians have the same rate of disease and suffer just the same as nonbelievers. It's just part of living in a fallen world. I have given my life to Christ, but I have a disease that will ultimately end my life early unless God intervenes.

I believe God is a good God who allows bad things to happen. God allows suffering, trials, and hard times to prepare us for future trials, to teach us to help others, and to develop and deepen our faith in Him. What matters is how we deal with this discipline. Do we trust Him completely? This reveals to God—and to ourselves—the true condition of our hearts.

So why doesn't God heal me? I cannot answer that question, but I do know that I have the choice to be angry about it or to trust that He has my best interests in mind. I also know that there are some things I cannot change in life, so what purpose would anger and bitterness hold for me? Instead, I want to focus on changing my attitude and perspective so that I can make a difference in other people's lives. I want to work at thriving! My goal and purpose of going through a transplant—besides living and being with my family—is to serve God and bring glory to His kingdom. It is my belief that I am not going through this in vain but that through this situation I will be able to help others, encourage them, and, most importantly, point them to Jesus so that they can find eternal life and true hope.

## Living with Purpose

My pastor/mentor once challenged me by asking whether I really believed that God is "all good." After all, he said, if I truly believed that God always had my best interests in mind, then why would I assume my desire for miraculous healing was better than what He has planned for me? When we worship God, not because of who He is but because of what He can do for us, that's idolatry. We see God as our magic genie and wait for Him to grant our wishes, and in so doing we worship ourselves more than Him. I am guilty of this. I have approached God many times for what He can do for me, not for who He is—Holy God, King of Kings, Lord of Lords, great I Am, Lion of Judah.

My pastor also challenged me because he noticed that I was developing a pattern of projecting fear into my future. There was a time when I believed that I did not have a future, so I didn't plan for one. That is a stupid way of thinking—one in which I was automatically predicting and foreshadowing failure for myself. Why would I want to predict such negativity for myself? If God in His infinite wisdom has decided that healing is not right for me, then I have to believe He has something brighter in mind to bring glory to His kingdom and joy to my life. I need to worship God for who He is, not for what He can do. When I ultimately achieve this, I am truly thriving.

I still pray every day for a miraculous healing of my body, but I also pray that the joy of the Lord will be inside me so I can make a difference in this world. God may heal me today, He may heal me tomorrow, He may heal me through this transplant, or He may not heal me at all while I am on this earth. Of course, I prefer that He would heal me sooner rather than later, but all I can do is continue to live my life with as much purpose and passion as I can. Just because I have a chronic disease does not mean my life should be without purpose—on the contrary, I feel it gives me even more reason to find new purpose and make a difference. I have purpose as a husband and father. I have purpose as a son and brother. I have purpose as a mentor to my friends and an example to others. I have purpose by writing this book and making a difference in the lives of readers. God has allowed me to have this amazing story, and it's my responsibility to use it and bring glory to His kingdom.

God pursues a relationship with all of us. By opening the door to Him, we accept His grace and love and gradually become more equipped to live fully for Him, for our loved ones and others, and for ourselves. I am not perfect or even strong. Far from it—I am weak and struggle with doubt and fear. But because I believe in Christ, I know that I can rely on someone greater than me and that He will give me hope and peace.

## God Is the Equation and the Answer

During our time on earth, we should focus less on our physical health (which is temporary) and more on our spiritual health (which is permanent). God can and still does heal, but we need to accept His sovereign plan if we are not healed and do the best with what time we have. This does not include getting caught up in bitterness and anger, but rather having hope and peace about what is to come.

I have spent a lot of time and energy on the spiritual side of living with a disease because it is a real issue for all of us. The battle can be wearying to the soul. I do not believe the day will ever come when I will have it all figured out, but neither can I imagine a time when I will just accept it and not pursue praying for healing. This is not to say that I will become a crazed zealot who believes he can heal himself through enlightenment or some new trendy remedy. It is not my goal to make everyone think God will heal us, but rather to allow Him to be a source of peace and joy in times of pain.

God is gracious and loving. You may get angry with Him at times, but remember that God is full of grace, which means that He loves you more than you can ever imagine. It's not your job to understand God; all He asks is that you trust in His plan. You need to live your life believing that He has your best interest at heart, learning through your experiences, and growing as a result. Remember the saying, "What does not kill you will make you stronger." If you have a chronic disease or disability and know that you will pass on from this earth because of it, then accept it and don't waste the rest of your days being angry over something you cannot control. Find someone, such as a pastor who believes the Bible is the true Word of God, to encourage you to work through your issues and struggles. God hears prayers, and praying is a great thing to do when you feel you are out of options. Likewise, if you are a caregiver of someone with a disease, then you have the responsibility to be Jesus to that person through praying, encouraging, helping, and having faith for that person when he or she is lacking it.

God fits into everything because He is the equation and the answer. He wrote the beginning, middle, and end of our story and wants us to follow Him regardless of our situation. God is involved in our lives, whether we want to admit it or not. The question is whether He is in our hearts.

## Chapter 8

# THE POWER OF HOPE

THE OTHER DAY I was watching the movie *Dying Young,* in which a young man was dying of cancer. He had been hiding the truth from his lover all along, and when she found out about his deception, she was bewildered as to why he would do such a thing. I could see and feel the fear in his eyes as he said to her, "I'm afraid." She responded, "Afraid of what?" He then made a comment that hit so close to home it took my breath away: "Afraid to hope."[5] What a powerful statement—and one so true for so many people.

What makes us afraid to hope? Is it because we fear we maybe let down if we get our expectations up? Do we fear giving ourselves a false sense of protection or reality? And what makes us lose hope? I know that in my own life, there have been moments when I have lost hope. One time after I had a heart test, I was anxious to hear the results. I stressed over it and assumed the worst—and, unfortunately, I was right. The doctors told me that I had pulmonary hypertension and needed to use oxygen all the time. It was a devastating blow to my ego and sense of self, and for a time I lost hope. However, as we will discuss in this chapter, there is a way to hold on to hope in even the darkest times.

## What Is Hope?

Before we can examine hope and understand why it is crucial for us to have, we need to understand exactly what hope is. To do this, we first need to tackle what it is not. In his book *A Future and a Hope,* Lloyd Ogilvie states that hope is not wishful thinking. It does not include a wish list of what we want.[6] For example, my nine-year-old daughter has quite an extensive wish list, which she'll tell you all about if you ask. I wish to win the lottery and live on the beaches of San Diego. This is not hope but rather a want.

Nor is hope yearning, which is basically extreme wishing. In fact, if we experience a prolonged period of disappointment for something we yearn for, it can destroy the essence of our hope. Hope is also not cheery optimism. It can produce an optimistic attitude within us, but this should not be construed as a replacement for hope. According to David Augsburger, "Hope is patient, active, trusting, waiting for what is not seen, not yet possessed, not yet received but claims it in faith."[7] Hope is possibility! It gives us the wisdom to see between fantasy and reality and to experience both without one contaminating the other. Hope takes us into the future and allows us to act despite our fear.

Hope allows us to visualize what cannot be seen—which strangely sounds a bit like faith. In fact, hope and faith are cousins; they often go hand in hand, yet they are still unique and separate entities. Hebrews 11:1 says, "Now *faith* is being sure of what we *hope* for and certain of what do not see" (emphasis added). Hope gives us sense of a brighter future and a renewed attitude toward life when circumstances around us seem dim. The person with hope has faith in the future, a connection with the present, and a confidence in tomorrow.[8]

Hope is also closely connected with love. In her book *Faith, Hope, and Love,* Emily Brunner explains that we live in the past by faith, the present by love, and the future by hope.[9] As J. I. Packer and Carolyn Nystrom note, "Christian hope…is the looking ahead to the fulfillment of the promises of God."[10] And in their book *Trusting God Again,* authors Glandion Carney and William Rudolf Long state the following about hope: "Without the ability to hope and dream, we humans are lost. Hope is what drives us on; it urges us to try once more, to smile again, to reach out for help, to continue to believe in people. Hope gives shape to our longings and direction to our everyday existence. When we hope, we believe that there is still a future, and that we will have a role to play in it."[11]

Hope is powerful. It has the power to get us out of bed when we are depressed, heal our emotions when we are hurt, push us beyond our limits when we need to move ahead, and keep us fighting when we need to stay in the battle. Hope will not permit us to give up when the world around us seems to be crumbling. It will give us strength when we need it the most. It is the one last thread that connects us to life when our bodies are giving out on us or we do not see a bright future. Hope gives us confidence in who we are and allows us to recognize that we can continue to fight the good fight.

Hope is the antithesis of despair. It's like the difference between love and hate. We have all heard that the line between love and hate can get blurred at times. Take a spouse in an abusive situation, for example. The spouse may be getting physically, verbally, sexually, or emotionally abused, yet the abused wife will not leave the relationship because she "loves" her husband. This so-called love is really a mask for fear. Maybe it's fear of the unknown, fear of not being cared for, fear of being alone, or fear of not having a job or place to go. It's all rooted in fear. Hope is the cure for fear.

## Restoring Hope

Earlier, I mentioned a mentoring relationship I had with a pastor at our church. At the time, I needed someone to talk to about the thoughts and feelings I was experiencing as I pursued various life-and-death choices. I was having difficulty with the concept of needing a transplant and the two-years-to-live diagnosis. I was losing hope. The pastor and I met once a week and discussed some of the emotional, spiritual, and mental battles that I was going through. As we did, he made some acute observations:

- I was having trouble believing that God had my best interests at heart.
- I was being judgmental of God because I was feeling that my way was superior to His.
- I was projecting fear into my future, not hope.
- I was taking too much responsibility for other people's reactions instead of allowing God to work through the situation as He saw fit.

My pastor hit the nail on the head on every one of these issues, and I was blown away by his observations. I realized that my doubt and skepticism had taken over my rationalization and common sense and that my fear was winning the battle inside me. No one had ever confronted me in this manner before, and I immediately recognized that he was accurate in his assessment and that I needed to make changes in my heart and mind. I had to bury these things and put them into the grave so that hope and faith could come alive in me. I had to replace these false beliefs and self-imposed lies with more positive thoughts and ways of thinking.

I gradually began to replace the hope-robbing thoughts with hope-giving thoughts. Here are some of the areas I addressed:

| Hope-Robbing Thoughts | Hope-Giving Thoughts |
| --- | --- |
| Control | Dependence on God and patience in His timing |
| Anger | Joy, contentment, and satisfaction with the situation (acceptance of CF and the transplant) |
| Fear | Peace, contentment, and learning to trust despite my circumstances |
| Guilt | Release from responsibility, forgiveness of self and others, freedom in allowing God to take over fears |

| Hope-Robbing Thoughts | Hope-Giving Thoughts |
|---|---|
| Doubt | Faith and freedom in God's love and His will |
| Pride (remember, this goes before a fall) | Humility, acceptance of myself and my qualities (good and bad) |

Most of us have to deal with these hope-robbing thoughts at one point or another in our lives. It's a daily battle of our souls, and we have to choose to replace these hope-robbing thoughts with hope-giving ones. Psalm 107:19-20 says, "Then they cried to the Lord in their trouble, and he saved them from their distress. He sent forth his word and healed them; he rescued them from the grave." We need to put these negative thoughts to death so that hope—its counterpart—can be brought to life.

I am scared to get a transplant. I know the risks, the possible side effects of the medications I will have to take, and the long-term implications of having the surgery. But I also know that I must hold onto hope and move forward. Once I allow fear to control me and make me lose hope, I fail at living as I was originally designed.

## The Road to Hopefulness

Hope has a place in every person's life, but it is even more important for those who are suffering from a disease. In fact, research suggests that hope plays a large part in the healing process. For years, psychologists have known that there is power when hope is integrated into the physical process of recovery. There are even assessments based on hope to evaluate if a patient has a better prognosis.

In one research study conducted by Robert Richardson, he found that patients suffering from chronic heart failure who were hopeful were able to maintain their involvement in life despite the physical limitations imposed by their condition. This hopefulness allowed his patients to live their lives more abundantly despite their prognosis. In another study using the Miller Hope Scale among heart transplant patients, findings showed that hopelessness was a strong predictor of adverse health outcomes.[12]

According to this research, hope is an indicator of an increased and improved lifestyle, while hopelessness is an indicator of adverse outcomes. Hope can transcend beyond the crisis or disease and give life even to the dying. While hope in itself does not heal a person, it does give that person more abundant life and brings peace when needed. Just because a lack of hope can cause an illness or make it worse does not mean that illness has to affect hope. Illness does not predict a change in hope; rather, true internal hope predicts a change in illness.

People who suffer from a physical disability have circumstances that often seem quite hopeless. Many are going back to the hospital for a new test or are waiting for a diagnosis or are worrying about results or are fearful that the worst news is yet to come. It's difficult in these life-and-death circumstances to embrace the path of hopefulness. However, although the road is not an easy one, when people choose to replace the hope-robbing thoughts with hope-giving ones and take the path of hope over the path of despair, it makes a huge difference in their situations.

I tell my students at school that the correct decision is not usually the easy one. As Robert Frost once wrote,

> "Two roads diverged in a wood, and I—
> I took the one less traveled by,
> And that has made all the difference."[13]

It's all too easy to take the road of despair, self-pity, and victimization and adopt a "woe is me" mentality. But taking the high road of hope has a lot more to offer than despair—and besides, it takes the same amount of energy anyway, so we really have nothing to lose.

## The Source of True Hope

In the Bible a man named Job had all types of adversity thrown at him. He lost his entire family, his wealth, his livelihood, and his health. He got angry and expressed to God his pain, his anguish, and even his wish to die. Now, there is nothing inherently wrong with expressing anger and grief—we all need our space and time to grieve and lament when we go through a difficult situation. Loss is universal among those with a disability, and we must grieve when we lose something. What matters is how we recover from that loss and ultimately move on. No matter how we get hit in life, we have to get back up and press on.

This does not mean that we walk around with a mask of fake joy on our face and tell everyone that we feel wonderful. That would be a lie. Hope stems from the internal soul and comes from our living Savior, Jesus. When times are difficult, we have to go in search of it and grasp hold of it. Hope is automatically given to us as Christians—it's a part of God's wonderful grace that He gives to us when we enter into His kingdom.

A song by Casting Crowns has brought me to tears many times in the midst of my storms. The song is called "Praise You in This Storm," and the chorus talks about how no matter what our storm is and how much we suffer, we are still called to praise God in that storm. He is God, and although life can be very difficult, He still loves us, and He will not leave us.

The Bible says that God sees our tears (2 Kings 20:5) and never leaves us (Deut. 31:6). This should provide a sense of peace and comfort to all of us because we know that God is aware of our tears and hard times. It's healthy for us to grieve our losses, but we must move on at some point and continue to fight the battle. If we linger in the grief process too long, it has the potential to turn our soul into something ugly and harmful. It takes us down a path of despair, and that's a deep and dark place from which it is difficult to escape.

Only when we, like Job, have experienced the death of hope can we grasp and hold on to hope. By knowing and feeling failure, fear, a negative test result, another diagnosis, and pain, we are able to grasp the concept of hope. Hope will fade when it is a *false* hope not rooted firmly in Christ. I see these false hopes all the time. People place their hopes in money, sex, a relationship, their jobs, their identity, and false religions. These are materialistic and superficial, have little to no depth, and will fade away. This is why we must have hope in Christ because other "hopes" are not true hope and will disappoint us. Romans 5:3-5 tells us that hope in Christ is the only hope that will not disappoint.

Of course, our hope in Christ does not guarantee that we will be cured from a disease or even live a pain-free existence. God does not promise a perfect life or that we will not endure trials and sufferings. But a hope in Christ does allow us to live with confidence and the assurance that God has promised He will give us a way out so that we can stand up under the pressures, attacks, and temptations of false hopes. As Paul writes in 1 Corinthians 10:13, "No temptation has seized you except what is common to man. And God is faithful; he will not let you be tempted beyond what you can bear. But when you are tempted, he will also provide a way out so that you can stand up under it."

## Helping the Hopeless

In Luke 4:18-19, Jesus says, "The Spirit of the Lord is on me, because he has anointed me to preach good news to the poor. He has sent me to proclaim freedom for the prisoners and recovery of sight for the blind, to release the oppressed, to proclaim the year of the Lord's favor." One way for us to restore hope and find purpose in life is to give back to those who are also suffering. Jesus was sent to help others, and we are called to do the same. We *are* our brother's keeper, and we can find purpose through being available to other people who are struggling.

If you are a person who suffers from a disease, you have greater awareness and empathy of other people's situations because you have walked in their shoes, felt their pain, heard the same bad news, waited for the next needle, and woken up not sure what the day would bring. One helpful activity I have undertaken recently is having lunch with David, a friend with a similar story as mine who just went through the transplant process. David was a huge encouragement to me because I know he walks in the same shoes as I do and understands my fears and reservations. He was willing to be vulnerable with me, open up about his story, and encourage me, which not only helped me but also gave him a purpose despite his story with CF. In a general sense, pain hurts whether it is physical, emotional, or relational, and so we all have something in common. You can be a support to others in the midst of your afflictions, and by doing so you can provide a sense of hope and purpose to those you touch.

Likewise, if you are a caregiver to someone who is going toward that dark place of hopelessness, it's important for you to be available to talk with him or her and be a source of encouragement and hope. When I was in the hospital, my wife never left my side. Despite my misery and despair, she was a rock and a cistern of hope. Many people want to rush in and provide answers, get angry with the doctors, or provide their own instructions on how to get better. Saying things like "pray more" or "have more faith" or "suck it up" are not always healthy for a person going through a crisis to hear and can quickly build up walls in the relationship.

In Philippians 3:10, Paul says that Christians should be in "the fellowship of sharing in his sufferings." No one is supposed to deal with life's issues alone. So when you see that loved one going down the wrong road of despair (which may appear as depression, sadness, overeating, under-eating, taking drugs or alcohol, addiction, erratic behavior, or an overall change in personality), that person may need you to be his or her source of hope because he or she is just not capable of being hopeful or feeling joy in that moment.

Remember, you have a living hope in God. He is no longer hanging on a cross but is alive within you when you accept a personal relationship with Him as your Savior, ask for forgiveness of your sins, and commit to follow Him. As Proverbs 3:6 states, "In all your ways acknowledge him, and he will make your paths straight." So do not give up hope for a miracle. I pray for a miracle to occur in my own life for two reasons: to have the glory of God shown and to grow old with my wife and family. Let's hope together!

*May the God of hope fill you with all joy and peace as you trust in him, so that you may overflow with hope by the power of the Holy Spirit.*

—Romans 15:13

*Chapter 9*

. . . . . . . . . . . . . . . . . . . . . . . . . . . . . . . . . . . . .

# EMBRACE THE MYSTERY

WHY ARE WE here? What is the meaning of life? Why does God allow certain things to happen? Why do good people suffer? Why can't I get a job? Why does my mother have cancer? Why does my child have cystic fibrosis? Why did my child die? *Why me?*

Have you ever asked any of these questions? What answer did you arrive at, or are you still searching? Let's face it: life is a mystery.[14] A mystery can be defined as "a religious truth that one can know only by revelation and cannot fully understand." Another definition is "something not understood or beyond understanding." We do not always understand why things happen the way they do, and our search for answers often leads us to places we wish we hadn't gone—places that lead us to more frustration and confusion. We can also become angry with God and blame Him for our misery and suffering, as if He were the cause. As I mentioned, I am guilty of this—I blamed God for not doing more to heal me. I tried so hard to understand the reasons why I had CF, but I could not grasp why I had to suffer and go through a transplant and ultimately ten surgeries just to have a chance at a longer life.

Unfortunately, we often have to accept the fact that we may never know the answers to our questions. Many times, we must just embrace the mystery of life. This is when healing occurs and we can begin to start the journey of finding our purpose and passion. As Christians who profess that Jesus Christ is Lord, accept Him as our Savior, and follow His Word, we must lay hold to the fact that God is good. We need to rely on that basic foundation and trust in it. This can be quite difficult to do, especially when we are in the midst of a terrible storm and are scared. As I wrote about earlier, fear is powerful. It is not something to be taken lightly, as it can captivate our hearts, become our spiritual nervous system, and control us.

## The Promise of Suffering

As I stated earlier, when my pastor reminded me that God does not give bad gifts but only good ones, I took that to heart and repeatedly said it to myself to grasp the concept at a heart level. God did not give me CF. He did not point His finger at me and speak a disease into my life. Sin did that when it entered the world. God is not the creator of disease and death, but rather He came so that we might have life and have it abundantly (see John 10:10). God does not inflict natural disasters or administer holocaust or genocide.

Regrettably, we live in a world full of evil and sin, and this evil rules this world, not goodness. In 2 Corinthians 4:4, Paul states, "The god of this age [Satan] has blinded the minds of unbelievers, so that they cannot see the light of the gospel of the glory of Christ, who is the image of God." This is not to say that God will not have His time and day. As John reveals in the book of Revelation, during the end times God will come to this earth again and ultimately win the war over evil. We can have hope in knowing that even though we may lose a battle here or there, the ultimate war is already won. We need to be on the winning side: in Christ's battle lines.

At times I find myself thinking, *Great, we ultimately will win the war…but how does this help me now?* It's like the soldier in the battle who knows he will ultimately win the war but at the same time is preoccupied with dodging the bullets that are flying at him. What's interesting is that God does not say we will not suffer in this world; actually, He said quite the opposite. In Romans 5:3-4, Paul says we are to "rejoice in our sufferings [which assumes we will all suffer], because we know that suffering produces perseverance; perseverance, character; and character, hope." Again, in Romans 8:18 he writes, "I consider that our present sufferings are not worth comparing with the glory that will be revealed in us." John 16:33 promises us that we will have troubles in this world.

The secret to having a successful life does not involve having a pain-free existence. Rather, it involves focusing our energy, heart, and soul on what is most important: Christ. If we can learn to live for God as fully devoted followers, we can learn to rejoice in the midst of our struggles. Revelation 17:14 says that when we follow Him, we are His "called, chosen and faithful followers." In Philippians 4:4, Paul says, "Rejoice in the Lord always. I will say it again: Rejoice!"

## The Thorn in Paul's Flesh

In Philippians 4:11-13, Paul writes, "I have learned to be content whatever the circumstances. I know what it is to be in need, and I know what it is to have plenty. I have learned the secret of being content in any and every situation, whether well fed or hungry, whether living in plenty or in want. I can do everything through him who gives me strength." Paul was one of the wisest examples and role models this world has ever known. God chose him. Any time we are God's chosen, we have the potential to make a difference.

Paul was no stranger to pain. He was shipwrecked, stoned, beaten, and imprisoned, yet he never lost sight of what was important. He also lived with some type of "thorn" in his flesh. No one knows for sure what this thorn was, but it was evidently somewhat severe and affected him greatly because he asked three times for it to be removed. (I don't imagine he would have pleaded with God on three separate occasions to remove a hangnail or a splinter.) In 2 Corinthians 12:7-10, Paul describes this condition:

> To keep me from being conceited because of these surpassingly great revelations [Paul had been having some amazing revelations from God that only he was privy to at the time], there was given

me a thorn in my flesh, a messenger of Satan, to torment me. Three times I pleaded with the Lord to take it away from me. But he said to me, "My grace is sufficient for you, for my power is made perfect in weakness." Therefore I will boast all the more gladly about my weaknesses, so that Christ's power may rest on me. That is why, for Christ's sake, I delight in weaknesses, in insults, in hardships, in persecutions, in difficulties. For when I am weak, then I am strong.

Each of us should be humbled when we read these words. In my own life, I know that I fail miserably in the department of rejoicing in my disease and weakness. I do a poor job of finding delight in hardships, persecution, and difficulties. Yet we are all instructed to hold firm in our faith despite suffering. In Revelation 2:10, God tells the church in Smyrna, "Do not be afraid of what you are about to suffer. I tell you, the devil will put some of you in prison to test you, and you will suffer persecution for ten days. Be faithful, even to the point of death, and I will give you the crown of life." God instructs us, His church, to be faithful to the end, and He promises that the result of our perseverance will be eternal life in His kingdom.

I view CF as my "thorn in the flesh" and find it difficult to live with, which is why I find comfort in knowing that Paul also wanted out of his affliction. He wanted an easier and less painful road. Most likely, however, his thorn made him even stronger in his ministry because those around him were able to witness the exemplary lifestyle he lived despite his affliction. His thorn probably humbled him by being a constant reminder that he was not in control and had to submit to a greater authority. His thorn may have even resulted in his staying in a place longer, which would have enabled him to build deeper relationships with the people in the community and with Christ.

Like Paul, I have asked God to remove CF, my "thorn in the flesh." Asking for an ailment, disease, or pain to be removed is never wrong, nor does it reflect a lack of faith. Even Jesus, the incarnate God, asked not to have to suffer on the cross. In Luke 22:42, as He was praying in the garden prior to Judas's betrayal, He said, "Father, if you are willing, take this cup from me." Jesus, the incarnate, sinless, blameless, and righteous one, asked for His "cup," the cross, to be taken away. Jesus knew it could not be taken away—He was sent to die for our sins—but He nevertheless still asked.

God tells us not to fear when we face difficult situations. In Exodus 20:20, Moses told the people, "Do not be afraid. God has come to test you, so that the fear of God will be with you to keep you from sinning." There is a purpose to the tests we are enduring: God is using them to humble us. We are not to be walking around boastful that we can do it all ourselves but rather to be humble in all we do. In Deuteronomy 8:2, Moses again says to the people, "Remember how the Lord your God led you all the way in the desert these forty years, to humble you and test you in order to know what was in your heart, whether or not you would keep his commands." God does not care as much about what our disease is, what we look like, or what job we have, as much as He cares about what is in our hearts.

Of course, this is not to say that we won't experience fear as we wait for that test result, diagnosis, or surgery. Waiting causes anxiety within us, which is to be expected, and we should embrace it. Some may assume that we lack faith because we are afraid or have anxiety, but I disagree. When Jesus asked to have His "cup" taken from Him, He said, "My soul is overwhelmed with sorrow to the point of death" (Matt. 26:38). He did not want to suffer the pain of the cross, but He was willing to do so because it was God the Father's will for His life.

The movie *The Passion of the Christ* gives us a picture of how brutal Roman crucifixions were and what Jesus endured for all of us. I don't know, nor will I surmise, whether Jesus was fearful, but it is clear that He did not want to walk down the road set for Him. I can understand not wanting to go through something that will bring about pain. I did not want to get a transplant, but I had to believe and have faith that this was what was best for my family, as God has created the opportunity for me to walk through that door. As my faith is tested, I can only pray that I will put God and His will first. My body and all that I have do not belong to me; God has blessed me enough to have them. I just hope and pray that He will continue to do a good work in me so that I can keep going a bit longer. I hope we can all follow suit with Jesus and, despite our fleshly desires, follow through with God's plan for our lives.

## Moving Past Questions to Actions

For many of us, the mystery is, "Why me?" or "Why now?" or "Why am I suffering from this?" Again, asking these types of questions is normal, but the problem comes when we get caught up and focus too much on the "why." At some point, we need to move on and focus on the "what"—what we need to do next. Such questions we need to ask are "What is the next step?" or "What does this mean for my family?" or "What do I need to learn from this?" We need to embrace these types of questions because when we deal with the "what," we will be motivated to act. It is our actions that will drive us toward thriving, not just asking why something is happening and feeling sorry for ourselves.

To do this, we must embrace the fact that why these things are happening to us is a mystery. The word *embrace* means "to take up especially readily or gladly," but it can also mean "the opportunity to study further."[14] This second definition caught me off guard, because it implies that embracing the mystery means to further study that which is not understood or beyond our understanding. Individuals with disabilities, along with their loved ones, should embrace their disability because the opposite is truly more detrimental. This may sound like a contradictory statement (and even a controversial one), but allow me to explain.

It's often helpful when attempting to understand a word or theory to first comprehend its counterpart. For example, we can have a better understanding of what "hot" means if we can comprehend what "cold" is. The opposite of embracing something is to reject it, which is what we typically do when faced with something we do not understand. We tend to ignore it, act as if it's not important, or convince ourselves that it does not matter to us. This is not possible or even healthy when we live with a disease. We are only hurting ourselves if we do not fully attempt to understand our disease or, at a minimum, learn from it and become wiser because of it. By ignoring it, rejecting it, or acting as if we do not have it, we only do ourselves harm. Denial and ignorance are not bliss.

In my own situation, I know that the more I focused on the "why" questions, the angrier I became because they caused me to entrench myself in self-pity and a "woe-is-me" attitude. I felt that I was entitled to know *why* I had CF and what God was going to do about it. This mentality took me down a slippery slope of despair, and once I hit the bottom of the ravine, it was difficult for me to climb out of it. I had to reorient my focus from the "why" to the "what," and this ultimately led me to identify the error in my thinking. I was getting caught up in thinking negatively and being angry with God, when I should have been saying, "I can do this. What's my next step?"

After meeting with my pastor and going through a few weeks of soul-searching and praying, I began to change my thinking pattern into more of an "I can do this" and "maybe things will be okay" attitude. I still struggle with this, and it's a constant battle in my mind and soul, but I know that I can conquer it by not choosing to give it power over me. Each of us must be soul-diers.

## Taking the Next Step

What do you need to embrace in your journey? What next step do you need to take to get yourself into a position where you feel good about yourself and are embracing the mystery? In my life, the next step I had to embrace was to get my arms—and my mind—around the idea of having a lung transplant. As I've mentioned, this was difficult for me to do because the statistics of survival from a lung transplant are somewhat grim (about a 50 percent survival rate at the five-year mark). To make matters worse, a friend of mine who had undergone the same surgery passed away because of complications from the new lungs. Ironically, the day I found out I was accepted for the transplant was the day I found out he had died.

How was I to embrace this? I could choose to be angry with God and allow that fear to creep back into my mind, or I could accept that I needed the surgery and do everything in my power to be as healthy as possible. I took the latter approach and joined a pulmonary rehabilitation program, where I rigorously exercised two hours each day three times a week. I tried to eat healthy and gain weight, since the long recovery time associated with the surgery often results in weight loss. I also realized that I needed to take vitamins and nutrients to stay healthy and fight infection. I delved into the Bible for encouragement. I started a Web site to share my experiences, feelings, fears, and successes with others. I had my small group and church pray for me, found a pastor/mentor to meet with, and tried to have a good attitude around my family. It was not easy, and I struggled with it daily, but I made the choice to do everything in my power to survive and thrive.

Taking that next step is a hard choice to make, but it will make all the difference for us and our loved ones. When we make the decision to embrace our diseases and fight the good fight, we also provide encouragement and hope to those around us. They begin to see a spark, and that spark can ignite into a roaring flame of hope and fortitude for everyone involved. Remember, when a person has a disease, it is not just his or her burden to carry but also his or her spouse's, children's, parents', friends' and extended family's burden. We are never alone, nor are we meant to be. We must allow ourselves to grieve our losses but then embrace the reality of our situation and move forward.

*Part IV*

# FIGHTING
# THE GOOD FIGHT

# Chapter 10

......................................................

# THE JOURNEY BEGINS

I WAS HAVING dinner at my favorite Mexican restaurant just outside of Pittsburgh with some friends and my brother on December 22, 2008. It was around 8:00 PM, and as my brother got up to leave, he said to me in a joking manner, "Make sure you don't get called [for the transplant] tonight because I have a lot to do tomorrow." Who says God does not have a sense of humor? Not more than five minutes later, my phone rang. It was an unknown number. I usually do not answer when I don't know the caller, but I figured I would answer it this time.

"Jason, this is Nancy," the voice said on the other end of the line. Nancy was my pre-transplant coordinator. "Merry Christmas, we have a set of lungs for you. You need to get to the hospital as soon as you can." I cannot even tell you the tornado of thoughts and feelings I had at that moment. I just sat there silently for a moment, gathering my nerves, and then I looked at my wife and said, "This is it." I knew at that moment that life would never be the same again.

I was shaking. As Natalie drove us home, I made phone calls to give out the alert to my friends and family to start praying. I arrived at the hospital at about 10:00 PM and was taken to a room on the transplant floor to get prepared. Things moved pretty quickly.

All I kept thinking was that once I went in for surgery, I might never see my wife and daughter again. I was pretty shaken and nervous, but I tried to appear calm on the outside (though my wife may disagree). I did not want to stress out my family by showing them how worried and anxious I truly was. I have become quite experienced over the years at maintaining a calm exterior when inside I am freaking out.

I was taken down to a pre-op waiting room, where I spoke to an anesthesiologist and the surgeon. At first, they were not sure if the lungs were going to be a match for me, since the other surgeons were at the site assessing them. After a few hours of waiting, we got the thumbs-up, and then life again seemed to move in fast-forward. The surgeon came in and said he would give my wife and me a few minutes alone, and then it would be time to operate. As I was being wheeled away, my wife asked me what I was thinking. I replied, "That God will never leave me or forsake me." These were words I would come to doubt and question over the next few months as my faith was tested over and over again.

## Surgery and Recovery

I slept well for the next eight and a half hours of surgery (I am thankful for anesthesia) while my family anxiously waited for news of the outcome. I really do not remember the next few days because I was pretty out of it, but the surgeon told my wife that the operation went well, though it did have its difficult moments. Due to thirty-two years' worth of infections and scar tissue, my left lung had deteriorated to nothing, which made it more difficult for the doctors to remove. My right lung was not as badly deteriorated, but due to its low level of functioning, they had their own fair share of difficulty in removing it.

I do remember waking up about twelve hours earlier than I was supposed to and being very alert while still intubated (having a tube down my throat to ensure that I could breathe). What I came to learn during my two-month stay in the hospital was that if I was told I would be sedated for twenty-four hours, I'd wake up in less than twelve. That became troublesome for me because I would wake up relatively alert but then discover a huge tube coming out of my mouth. I was unable to communicate with the doctors and nurses that I wanted the tube taken out.

Of course, I am not always the best patient either, especially when I am confused and disoriented. During one such incident, I woke up in the ICU much earlier than the doctors had planned, and of course the tube agitated me. It was really bothering me, so I reached up to move it over a bit. Suddenly, the nurse came in, screaming and threatening to tie me down if I tried to pull it out. I do not take well to threats under such conditions—especially given the fact that I was not trying to remove it—and when it finally did come out and I could talk again, I let that nurse know what I thought of her outburst. She later apologized. As I went through more and more surgeries, I developed hand motions (not always good ones) to communicate my desire to have the tube pulled out.

Within seven days of my transplant, I was up and walking almost a mile. Natalie and I did countless walks up and down the hallways of the transplant floor. I grew tired of that hallway, but walking was the best thing for me to do to get my new puffers working and to prevent any clots or further muscle loss. It was about a week after the transplant that things began to take a nosedive.

## Setbacks

I won't go into all the details, but I had ten surgeries within six weeks due to bowel obstructions and vocal cord injuries (the latter came about as a result of the numerous intubations). The bowel obstructions were difficult and painful to deal with. Although they can occur after any surgery, in my case they were much more severe. The doctors were courteous enough to inform me, more than once, that they had not seen this level of severity before in a patient.

Let me also interject here that during my two month "staycation" in the hospital, I missed Christmas, my fifth-year anniversary, New Year's Day, and Valentines Day. My wife was so incredible to stay day and night with me for the entire duration. I thank God that He gave me the foresight to buy Natalie's anniversary gift prior to all this occurring, so I was able to give it to her while in the hospital. I think it earned me a lot of good husband points. I can say with complete confidence that I am here today because of my wife and her supportive role during my hospitalization. During those days when I wanted to quit, she encouraged me to keep fighting.

Having a double-lung transplant and multiple bowel surgeries caused me quite a bit of pain. The trick to ease the pain was in taking narcotics (prescribed, of course). The catch-22 in my case was that the narcotics slowed down my bowels, which was not a good thing when I was already fighting the obstruction issues. These obstructions caused me immense pain at times, and I wanted relief, but the doctors were hesitant to give me the narcotics because of this unfortunate side effect. In most people, these obstructions could be alleviated with medications, laxatives, and enemas, but, again, I was not so lucky (though I had my share of enemas). My wife told me at one point that I looked like I was six months pregnant because my stomach was so distended from the obstruction. At times the pain level was ten out of ten, and it lasted for hours. Overall, I had six major surgeries on my intestines. During one surgery, the surgeon reported that I almost died on the operating table.

After one surgery, I woke up in the ICU and looked down at my stomach and began to panic. All I saw was this huge black bubble-looking contraption sticking out of my stomach. As it turned out, my intestines were too swollen after the surgery for the doctors to close me back up again, so they inserted a sponge into my stomach with a tube to drain all the fluid in hopes that my bowels would relax and the swelling would decrease enough for them to close me back up. I, of course, saw this sponge and thought it was my skin. I wondered what in the world had gone wrong. Fortunately, my wife read my mind and my panicked look and affirmed that it was only temporary. That gave me some relief, though not a whole lot. The risk of infection was huge due to my stomach remaining open, and the docs were very concerned that I may not survive.

After my last bowel operation, I asked the surgeon whether this would happen again. He replied, "It can't because you will not survive another surgery." Let's just say that I called on the prayer soul-diers even more to kick it up a notch. Never in a million years would I have thought that a lung transplant would result in six bowel surgeries and three vocal cord surgeries. Fortunately, my lungs were doing great!

The vocal cord surgeries were needed because my cords had been damaged by the multiple intubations I had received during the surgeries. For weeks afterward I couldn't talk or swallow. I learned to become a very good listener for the simple reason that for three weeks I couldn't speak. Maybe this was God's way of teaching me to listen more and talk less. I think He could have found an easier way…but then again, often I don't get the hint.

Due to my vocal cords not functioning properly and the bowel obstructions, I was not allowed to eat anything for two months, which resulted in severe weight loss and a heightened state of frustration and anxiety. This was very difficult for me because I continually received bad news that the surgeries did not work or that I needed another one, and I was desperate for some good news. I was hungry, and the ability to eat would have really boosted my spirits. The doctors were concerned that I would throw up and that my vomit would enter my lungs and do major damage, so they gave me a nasogastric tube to pull everything out of my stomach. The tube was horrible. It hurt going in and coming out, but more than that, I hated what it represented. I became rather obstinate after a few weeks of not eating, as I am sure you can understand.

I was fed by total parenteral nutrition (TPN), which means that they fed me through my IV and put enteral feedings into a tube, called a J-tube, that provided me with some nourishment. However, it gave me no relief from the hunger, since all the nutrition bypassed my stomach. Overall, I lost thirty pounds during the three months when I had the feeding tube.

I asked my doctor to pull the tube out once I returned home. She did so reluctantly, because she was concerned that I would not be able to gain the weight back. I am glad to say that as of the date of this writing, I have put back on the thirty pounds I lost.

## Home

I was released from the University of Pittsburgh Medical Center on February 16, 2009—my daughter's ninth birthday. When I went in for the transplant, I had every intention of being the fastest dischargee in history, but God had a different agenda. As every week passed and every surgery occurred, I truly wondered if I would ever leave that hospital alive. The doctors and surgeons kept saying, "Just a few more days," but then something would happen to extend my stay to a few more days...and then a few more days after that.

By the beginning of February, as you could imagine, I was feeling pretty rough and very low. After ten surgeries, immense pain, and repeated failures, I was very depressed and angry. My wife and I made the deal that we would do everything possible to leave by our daughter's ninth birthday because there was nothing I wanted to do more than be at home with her for that wonderful occasion. We told the doctors in early February that we wanted out by February 16, and, of course, I tried to bargain for an earlier release date (which didn't happen). Praise God, though, we were able to leave on my daughter's birthday.

After my discharge, we stayed in Pittsburgh with my folks for five weeks. My parents graciously sacrificed their first-floor bedroom for us (stairs were out of the question for me at the time). It was an emotional homecoming. My daughter made a banner welcoming me home and had it displayed across the entire garage door. We postponed her party a week so that I would have the strength to attend. It was a gala event of pizza, Dairy Queen ice cream cake (of which I ate three slices because I could not eat solid foods yet), and swimming. I was a spectator during the swimming component due to my lack of energy and strength and all the sutures I had. Still, it was wonderful to be together again as a family and to be reunited with my daughter.

Finally, the doctors gave us the thumbs-up to return home to South Carolina. Be it ever so humble, there's no place like home.

## Chapter 11

# THE SOUL-DIER

IN THE PREVIOUS chapter, I shared a bit about the journey my family and I have been on since I went in for the transplant surgery. I mentioned that not eating for two months was a difficult issue for me. Another very difficult issue I had to deal with was the deep feeling of hopelessness I experienced during my hospitalization. Even though I have learned to replace hope-robbing thoughts with hope-giving thoughts (as I described in chapter 8), this was an extremely difficult situation. You will never find me judging or criticizing anyone for feeling hopeless while in the throes of difficulty. Hopelessness is a very real entity for people, and I, too, experience it firsthand. Hope is always something we should be working toward and is a worthwhile journey where the ends do justify the means.

I was able to handle the physical aspects of the surgeries and pain (though at times it was overwhelming), but I struggled with believing there would ever be a light at the end of the tunnel and that things would turn out okay. Even though I had thousands of people praying for me all across the country, I did not sense that God was hearing the prayers. When Jesus was suffering on the cross, He cried out, "My God, my God, why have you forsaken me?" (Matt. 27:46). This is how I felt, and despite the hundreds of cards, e-mails, notes, and phone calls I received, encouraging me with Scriptures and words of promises, I had trouble believing God was with me. I imagined God up in heaven, just hanging out and watching me suffer, saying, "A little more," and I had no clue why He would allow this to occur.

Hebrews 5:7 says, "During the days of Jesus' life on earth, he offered up prayers and petitions with loud cries and tears to the one who could save him from death, and he was heard because of his reverent submission." I spent many days and nights crying out for compassion and mercy, but I did not *feel* or sense God's presence. I felt abandoned. I knew in my mind that God was with me, but I sure did not sense or feel He was there.

When I had the energy to walk longer distances, Natalie and I would go down to the hospital chapel, where I would break loose out of pure frustration and start crying out to God. I wanted to know where He was and why He wasn't doing more to help me or provide me with relief. I remember saying, "Why aren't You taking away this pain?" I was having an intense inner battle. I knew that I should have more faith, but because I was not seeing any signs of improvement, my faith was greatly lacking, and my anger level was rising. I remember asking Natalie why God was not intervening.

I began to get annoyed by all the cards I was receiving because they were all about hope and believing. Friends and family would say, "Keep the faith," "Have hope," "Keep trusting in God," "Be strong," and "God does not leave us." Now, don't get me wrong, I appreciated every one of those cards and e-mails, and I still have them all in a notebook. But at the time I was not all that fond of God, and I did not want to hear the Christian lingo. There were times when I literally cursed Him out and told Him that I would be better off without Him.

At one point I told my wife that I wanted to die. This is something no spouse should ever have to hear, but in that moment I was so tired of the pain, so tired of the fear, so tired of just being tired. I had reached the place where I did not believe the pain would ever ease, and therefore I had given up the will to continue the fight to live. I wanted to get out of that hospital and go home. I wanted the benefit of my new lungs without the pain of going through the process. My reality—although reality is often subjective and not reality at all—was the feeling that I was receiving the opposite of what I was praying for. I had prayed for no more surgeries, but then ended up having ten in all. I had prayed for relief, but I continued to have severe pain. I had prayed for an early release from the hospital, but I was there for sixty days. I prayed that I would pass the swallowing test that would allow me to eat, but I failed it four times. I had prayed for God to give me some sort of sign that He was present, but I didn't see it. Of course, that's not to say He was not there; I just did not sense Him.

## Tunnel Vision

I think it's safe to say that when we are in the midst of pain and suffering, our vision—our goggles—can get skewed and not give us an accurate perception of reality. We can get so self-focused that we fail to see the big picture. This is what I was struggling with while I was in the hospital. I knew that God was there, and I never stopped praying, but there were times when I stopped believing in Him. I was angry that an all-powerful God was not doing more for me in the crisis. I was feeling entitled to a miracle. After all, I was a God-fearing, born-again Christian who read the Bible, tithed, went to church, helped others, led a small group, and generally tried to be a good person.

However, as I mentioned earlier, the reality is that the only thing I was actually entitled to—without grace—was death. My actions were meaningless unless my heart was pure and I was earnestly seeking His will for my life and living for Him. As Paul says in Romans 3:23 and 6:23, we are all sinners, and the wages of sin is death, but I was not ready for that quite yet. It's a good thing that Christ died on the cross for us so that I might have a chance to live here on earth (a little longer now due to my new lungs) and in eternity with Him. This is the perspective I needed to have—the one in which God is good, loves me, does not forsake me, and shows compassion to me, although it might be in a different form than I had hoped. Philippians 2:13 says, "For it is God who works in you to will and to act according to his good purpose." God had a good purpose for me, and I needed to always remember that.

I truly experienced the lowest of the lows while I was in the hospital. I was standing in the midst of a storm, and all I could see were the dark clouds and the winds howling around me. I was feeling hurt and pain, and that was all I could see. We all have our share of hurts and pains in this life. One thing I struggle with is when people are sharing a current emotional, relational, physical, or spiritual pain they are going through and say, "I'm dealing with this issue…but, of course, it's nothing compared to what you have to put up with." Let me just say that pain is *pain*. Your pain, my pain, and a loved one's pain are all pain. It's never easy, and it all hurts. There may be varying degrees of pain, but when we are in the storm, that's all we can see. Fortunately for us, God stands above the storm and can see the big picture. Although our vision is limited, God's is not. We have to learn to trust Him and be obedient to Him, all while believing in His promises.

As humans, we tend to have tunnel vision and see only what's in front of us. It's as if we are standing in a large box. All we see as we look around are the walls of the box. We can look up and see out the top, but we cannot see what is going on beyond the four walls. We need to believe that God is looking outside of the box on our behalf and is directing the events we cannot see in order to shape our lives. If we believe in God and His promise that He loves us, we can continue to grow in our faith and begin a new journey. As we grow more obedient in doing this, the sides of the box will slowly start to come down, and we will begin to see our circumstances as God sees them.

I was in the box in the hospital and my walls consisted of pain, hopelessness, and suffering. I did not (and still do not) know what God was doing outside of my box because I was unable to see how He sees. I had to trust that God is a loving God and that He had my best interests in mind. First Corinthians 2:9 says, "No eye has seen, no ear has heard, no mind has conceived what God has prepared for those who love him." James 1:12 says, "Blessed is the man who perseveres under trial, because when he has stood the test, he will receive the crown of life that God has promised to those who love him." I had to believe that by loving God—which means having trust, obedience, faith, loyalty, and reverent fear of Him—and entering into a personal relationship with Him, I would receive the crown of life that He has promised to each of us.

First John 3:1 states, "How great is the love the Father has lavished on us, that we should be called children of God! And that is what we are!" I love the exclamation point in this verse because it indicates that God is ultraserious about this promise of love. He loves us so much that He calls us His children. I know that when my daughter is sick or having a tough time, it's hard to watch her suffer. Yet this does not even come close to the magnitude of which God cares for us.

## The Silver Lining

It's good to live life with purpose, but it's also necessary to find passion in life. After I go through a trial, I try to look for a silver lining or a way to use what I learned during the trial to make a difference in someone else's life. I never want to go through a trial in vain. I want to be able to honestly reply to anyone I encounter who claims, "You would not understand," with "Yes, I do!" I have been angry at God, I have been down the road of despair, I have wanted to die, I have lost all hope, and I have given up my will to fight. Knowing I can use this to be an encouragement and support to those who go through difficult times gives me the freedom to accept the trials I have gone through.

I believe God puts trials in our lives so we can learn lessons and be equipped to support and help others. I know my story has helped many people, and this means much more to me than just having new lungs (although I sure do like them). It's just like my donor family who lost a loved one. I recently wrote a letter expressing my gratefulness to them for giving me a second chance at life. I told them that the death of their loved one had not been in vain but had brought new life. Because of my donor's death, I now have the chance to continue being a father, husband, son, brother, and friend. My hope is that a relationship will form between us and that my life will serve as a positive memory of their loved one.

As I write this chapter, I am sitting in the cancer ward of the hospital getting an infusion of some antibody that my blood results indicated I was low of. I sit here knowing how these people feel and probably what they are thinking. My heart breaks for them as I watch them get infusions of chemotherapy. I pray for their minds to be solid and their hearts to be strong as I watch them getting IV lines put in for their infusions of chemotherapy. I saw the fear in some patients and the resilience in others. I know that some are thinking, *What next? How can I keep doing this? Will I be here for my kid's next birthday? How will my spouse move on without me?* These are thoughts I had—and still have—and because I share these thoughts with them, I can empathize with their situation. For me, this is the silver lining in the trials I have endured.

In his book *The Last Lecture,* Randy Pausch shared how he wanted to live his last few months after being diagnosed with pancreatic cancer. He struggled with knowing that his young children would grow up without him and that he would soon have to leave his wife, but he chose to focus on what he had during his remaining time on earth instead of on what he would lose. We all have a similar choice to make: we can focus on despair or try to look for the positive in our situation. In my case, when I was in the hospital, my wife encouraged me to get out and walk every day. There were many times when I just wanted to lie in bed and wallow in my misery, but my love for my wife and my desire to live with her and my daughter gave me just enough strength to get out of bed every day and keep fighting (although begrudgingly).

Before the transplant, I started a Web site to journal and blog my way through what was going to happen. I wanted to be vulnerable so that others would learn about transplants and organ donations. I wanted those who were going to go through the same surgery as I to use my experience and learn from it. I also wanted to make a difference in others' lives by sharing my story and being a support to them. Yes, I went through many difficult times and had a lot of pain, but I made it though. God gave me the strength to endure, and I believe He gives that same strength to everyone who needs it.

## Choosing to Live

In the hospital I had a choice about how I would deal with my situation. Sometimes I chose to be angry at God, and other times I chose to trust in Him. Trusting in Him was difficult to do when my pain level was a ten out of ten and all I kept hearing from the doctors were negative reports. While I do not believe that we should blame God for every negative thing that occurs to us, it's often quite easy to do because, after all, He is God.

At one point, my pastor came to visit me in the hospital, and I looked at him and said, "I cannot do this anymore. I can't keep praying." He replied that I did not have to. He said that thousands of soul-diers were praying for me and that they had my back. He told me it was okay to have doubts and question my faith. His response brought me a sense of peace. I did not have to show toughness and do things on my own. I believe that the only reason I am here today is because of the prayers and support of others. I'm thankful to my doctors, nurses, and surgeons who never gave up on me. I'm thankful to my family and the many prayer soul-diers who prayed for me even when things seemed grim. When I gave up and stopped fighting, they all stepped in and fought for me. When I was hopeless, they were hopeful despite the odds. When the doctors said I would need another surgery and I became afraid, they kept the faith. They saw the glass half full when I saw it completely empty. The community of friends and family around me allowed me to find a sense of peace that I was not alone and did not have to do it all by myself.

Fear is a powerful emotion. It can motivate us to fight, or it can debilitate us and cause us to want to run and hide. I believe that God has placed within each of us the ability to fight fear, but often when we experience repeated trials, we lose hope and allow fear to get the upper hand. We begin to believe that we cannot fight the battle. This is a lie, but we accept it as truth. Instead, when we are faced with loss or potential loss, we need to dig down deep and find that area in our hearts that knows we are souldiers. We need to fight for ourselves and our loved ones, because they are worth it.

As Christians, we know that we have the tools we need to fight because we are blessed to have the Holy Spirit living within us, who provides us with our source of counsel, peace, joy, and hope. In Romans 5:5, Paul tells us that "hope does not disappoint us, because God has poured out his love into our hearts by the Holy Spirit, whom he has given us." In John 14:16, we learn that God has given us this wonderful Counselor (Helper) to be with us forever. We also discover in John 14:26 that this "Counselor, the Holy Spirit, whom the Father will send in my name, will teach you all things and will remind you of everything I have said to you." This means that we have the Holy Spirit inside us not only to help us through the hard times but also to remind us of God's promises. In Psalm 119:49-50, David says, "Remember your word to your servant, for you have given me hope. My comfort in my suffering is this: Your promise preserves my life."

## God Will Never Forsake Us

As I mentioned previously, when I was being wheeled into surgery for my transplant, I told Natalie that God would not forsake me. Even though I did not sense God for a long time, I chose to believe that His Word was truth and that He had promised never to abandon me (see Heb. 13:5). Just as He promised that He would never flood the world again (see Gen. 9:11), He also promises that He will never abandon His children.

God tells us in 2 Timothy 1:7 that He "did not give us a spirit of timidity, but a spirit of power." So when you are faced with a trial, you need to focus on the spirit of power that you have been given and reject the spirit of timidity and fear. You need to face the battle as a soul-dier and "fight the good fight of the faith" (1 Tim. 6:12). As Paul says in Ephesians 5:15-16, "Be very careful, then, how you live—not as unwise but as wise, making the most of every opportunity." You have no idea how many days you have left on this earth, which is why I encourage you to live each day with purpose and passion. Enjoy those you love and spend quality time with them.

Men, take the time to be the husband and dad you were called to be. Love your wife as Christ loved the church (see Eph. 5:25). Wives, be the godly women you were chosen to be and support your husbands and children with unconditional love. Above all, the most important thing you can do here on this earth is to "love the Lord your God with all your heart and with all your soul and with all your strength" (Deut. 6:5). Jesus says that this is the first and greatest commandment, and the next greatest command we are given is to "love your neighbor as yourself" (Matt. 22:39).

Fearing God, following His commands, claiming His promises, and living the life you have been purposed to live will provide you with life even if you are facing death. Living with disease and disabilities is difficult, and there will be times of immense pain, suffering, and hopelessness. There will be times when you will want to give up, but remember that you have been called to fight the good fight. You can find joy, purpose, and passion in this world, even when your physical body seems to be crumbling. You can find true joy, even when you are angry or hurting and desperately want relief. You can find purpose by drawing on your trials and experiences to help others, even though it might not seem possible at the time.

This is never easy, and we will have successes and failures as we are called to fight as soul-diers each day. But ultimately we can thrive!

*I encourage you to review my Web site at www.thesouldier.com. Please feel free to e-mail me or leave a comment in the blog section; I would love to hear from you. If you are interested in having me come speak to your church, organization, business, or nonprofit organization, please contact me via my Web site. I will customize a presentation specific to your needs.*

# ENDNOTES

## Introduction

1.  "Disability Information and Statistics," *Joni and Friends International Disability Centre: http://www.joniandfriends.org/ disability_stats.php* (April 14,2010).

## Chapter 1

2.  "Disability Information and Statistics," *Joni and Friends International Disability Centre: http://www.joniandfriends.org/ disability_stats.php* (April 14,2010).

## Chapter 2

3.  http://www.cff.org/AboutCF/
4.  Rejection occurs as a result of the body not accepting the transplant organ. This occurs when the immune system of the recipient attacks the new organ.

## Chapter 8

5.   The movie *Dying Young* was filmed in Redwood, California. It was released by Twentieth Century Fox Film Corporation and Fogwood Films in 1991. It was written by Marti Leimbach, and the screenplay was by Richard Friedenberg.
6.   Lloyd John Ogilvie, *A Future and a Hope* (Nashville, TN: Word, 1988).
7.   David Augsburger, *When Enough Is Enough: Discovering True Hope When All Hope Seems Lost* (Scottdale, PA: Herald, 1984).
8.   Ibid.
9.   Emil Brunner, *Faith, Hope, and Love* (Philadelphia, PA: Westminster, 1956).
10.  J. I. Packer and Carolyn Nystrom, *Knowing God Through the Year* (Downers Grove, IL: InterVarsity, 2004).
11.  Glandion Carney and William Rudolf Long, *Trusting God Again: Regaining Hope After Disappointment or loss* (Downer's Grove, IL: InterVarsity, 1995).
12.  Robert Richardson, "When There Is Hope, There Is Life: Toward a Biology of Hope," *Journal of Pastoral Care* 54 (2000): 75-83.
13.  Robert Frost, "The Road Not Taken," in *Mountain Interval* (New York: Henry Holt, 1920).

## Chapter 9

14.  Merriam-Webster® Dictionary, s.v. "Embrace," *http://www.merriam-webster/dictionary/embrace.*